John Stuart Mill

autobiography of
JOHN STUART MILL

WITH A FOREWORD BY
ASA BRIGGS

A SIGNET CLASSIC

PUBLISHED BY THE NEW AMERICAN LIBRARY

FOREWORD COPYRIGHT © 1964 BY THE NEW AMERICAN
LIBRARY OF WORLD LITERATURE, INC.

First Printing, October, 1964

SIGNET TRADEMARK REG. U.S. PAT. OFF. AND FOREIGN COUNTRIES
REGISTERED TRADEMARK—MARCA REGISTRADA
HECHO EN CHICAGO, U.S.A.

SIGNET CLASSICS *are published by*
The New American Library of World Literature, Inc.
501 Madison Avenue, New York, New York 10022

PRINTED IN THE UNITED STATES OF AMERICA

TABLE OF CONTENTS

FOREWORD

Most autobiographies are concerned with lives of action, usually either in politics or in war. John Stuart Mill's *Autobiography*, however, deals with the development of a mind, with the origin of ideas and their impact, and with the interplay of education and experience. Thomas Carlyle found it dull, "little more human in it than if it had been done by a thing of mechanized iron"; yet just as Mill has outlasted Carlyle as a thinker and a writer, so the *Autobiography* has outlasted most of Carlyle's works.

It is interesting and illuminating, as Mill hoped that it would be, for two reasons. First, it reveals the way in which Mill himself formed and changed his opinions and attitudes; and since Mill's opinions and attitudes are of strategic importance in nineteenth-century intellectual history, the *Autobiography* is a major source. Second, it has a representative quality. Mill wrote on his opening page, "in an age of transition in opinions, there may be somewhat both of interest and of benefit in noting the successive phases of any mind which was always pressing forward, equally ready to learn and to unlearn either from its own thoughts or from those of others." Concerned as it is throughout with a remarkable "age of transition" in English history and with many of the circles of thinkers who set out to interpret or to mould the age, the *Autobiography* is as important a document for the understanding of the nineteenth century as it is for the understanding of Mill himself.

There is no doubt that Mill conceived of the *Autobiography* as a didactic agency which might contribute towards the formation of other people's opinions rather than as a full self-revelation or confession. "One does not, in writing a life, either one's own or another's, undertake to tell everything," he wrote to his wife in February, 1854. A few days earlier he had written to her about "the sacred duty of fixing in writing ... everything that I have in my mind which is capable of assisting the destruction of error and prejudice and the growth of just feelings and true opinions." Few autobiographies have been written quite in this spirit. There is more in common, indeed, between the purpose of the *Autobiography* and the purpose of most of Mill's other writings than between the purpose of the *Autobiography* and that of most other autobiographies.

It was not simply that Mill's life was "uneventful," as he himself described it. Given the uneventfulness, Mill quite deliberately chose to leave out of his account much that other writers would have put in. He had a highly developed sense of what was relevant and what was irrelevant to his main purpose. In particular, he rarely dwelt on his loves or hates. He acknowledged most of his intellectual debts without fully revealing his human interests or ranging completely over his public activities. Much that might have been central is either missing or becomes background. For this reason alone, the *Autobiography* needs to be supplemented both by letters and by other people's accounts of his life.

The main facts in Mill's life provide a simple scaffolding, and the most important facts, at least in Mill's own opinion, relate to books. Mill was nearly fifty years old when the first draft of the *Autobiography* was written between 1853 and 1856. He died in 1873, the year of publication of the final version. Two of his most influential books had already been written before he turned to his own life—*A System of Logic, Ratiocinative and Inductive* (1843) and *Principles of Political Economy* (1848). Between 1856 and 1873 he published, among other works,

On Liberty (1859), *Considerations on Representative Government* (1861), *Utilitarianism* (1863), and *The Subjection of Women* (1869). He also collected four volumes of articles and reviews under the title *Dissertations and Discussions*. These included brilliant and penetrating studies of Bentham and Coleridge and a number of well-informed papers on political and intellectual currents in Europe.

Mill mentions most of these writings in the *Autobiography,* setting them, indeed, within the framework of contemporary debate. He preferred writing about these subjects to talking about them. He complained feelingly in his *Autobiography* that all serious discussions on "matters on which opinions differ" was treated as "ill-bred" in the England of his day. At the same time, what was written could command a growing audience. It was to that audience that the *Autobiography,* like Mill's other books, was addressed. As he wrote in his essay *On Liberty,* "Never when controversy avoided the subjects which are large and important enough to kindle enthusiasm was the mind of a people stirred up from its foundations, and the impulse given which raised even persons of the most ordinary intellect to something of the dignity of thinking beings." The statement of how his own mind developed, therefore, must be related to Mill's views on the development of "the mind of a people."

The other facts concerning Mill explain why he was able to write so much and a good deal of what he actually wrote. He was born in 1806, the eldest of the nine children of James Mill, the Utilitarian philosopher and Radical reformer. His education, to which many pages of the *Autobiography* are devoted, was one of the most remarkable in modern times. He was taught Greek at the age of three and Latin at the age of seven, logic at twelve, and political economy at thirteen. The result was that during his childhood, if it could be described as a childhood, he imbibed "an amount of knowledge in what are considered the higher branches of education, which is seldom acquired (if acquired at all) until the age of manhood." In one of his most picturesque sentences he concludes, "I started, I may fairly say, with an advantage of a quarter of a century over my contemporaries."

The early part of the *Autobiography* tells us as much

about James Mill as about his son. James Mill's views
on education were carefully formulated and grounded in
principle. He believed in losing no time, in covering an
immense stretch of ground, and in making his son understand, as far as he was able, the principles which he believed constituted a new framework of knowledge. Yet
he left out almost completely the practical side of life,
ignored religion, and relied to a quite considerable extent
on fear as an incentive. John Stuart Mill's comments on
all these points are brief but informative. "The education
which my father gave me was in itself much more fitted
for training me to know than to do." "I am thus one of
the very few examples, in this country, of one who has not
thrown off religious belief, but never had it: I grew up in
a negative state with regard to it. I looked upon the
modern exactly as I did upon the ancient religion, as something which in no other way concerned me." "The element which was chiefly deficient in his [James Mill's]
moral relation to his children was that of tenderness."

John Stuart Mill's position among his contemporaries
can only be fully understood if these three "deficiencies"
of his education are taken into account as well as the lead
in time that he gained over them. The mid-Victorian age,
when Mill was in his prime, was intensely practical, with
heated religious debate preoccupying intelligent and un-
intelligent people alike, and with a thick coating of sentimentality covering opinions and relationships. Mill did
not want to accommodate himself to his age but to direct
it, and he often lamented his isolation. "With us," he wrote
in a famous passage in *On Liberty,* "heretical opinions do
not perceptibly gain, or even lose, ground in each decade
or generation; they never blaze out far and wide, but continue to smoulder in the narrow circles of thinking and
studious persons among whom they originate, without ever
lighting up the general affairs of mankind with either a
true or deceptive light."

Yet Mill's account of his education is not simply a rational statement of profit and loss which can be tested in
the balance sheet of his life. It hides deep emotion. In a
rejected early draft of the *Autobiography* Mill complained
that he grew up with a strong sense of reserve, a lack of
spontaneity, and a dangerous habit of "leaving my re-
sponsibility as a moral agent to my father, my conscience

never speaking to me except by his voice." A comparison of the published version of the *Autobiography* with the early drafts, recently edited by Jack Stillinger, brings out many fascinating points about Mill's changing approach to self-evaluation. The various versions of the *Autobiography* demonstrate what Professor Stillinger calls a "progress from private to public, and from public to more public, voice." What begins by being highly personal in the first drafts is generalized in the later drafts: psychological notes acquire the objective mould of generic case studies. In the light of detailed exegesis, it is impossible to agree with Professor Basil Willey's view in *Nineteenth Century Studies* (1949) that the early chapters of the *Autobiography* "amply confirm" Carlyle's comprehensive indictment of its dullness. Nothing is more misleading than Carlyle's comment, "autobiography of a steam engine, perhaps, you may sometimes read it."

Mill's famous "crisis" in his early manhood was directly related to the education he had received. Before he deals with the crisis, however, in what all critics agree is a most interesting Chapter V, Mill sets other aspects of his early "mental development" in orderly perspective. When he was fourteen, he spent a year in France in "the free and genial atmosphere of Continental life." He lived there with the brother of his father's closest friend, Jeremy Bentham, but he read widely many books which fell outside the usual range of English argument. "The chief fruit which I carried away from the society I saw," he wrote in the *Autobiography,* "was a strong and permanent interest in continental Liberalism, of which I ever afterwards kept myself *au courant,* as much as those of English politics; a thing not at all usual in those days with Englishmen."

Scholarly essays could be written on Mill's relationship with three French thinkers whose mental paths often crossed his own—Saint-Simon, de Tocqueville, and Comte. There is certainly far more to be said about the nature and unfolding of these relationships, particularly the relationship with de Tocqueville, than is said in the *Autobiography*. The passage in the *Autobiography* praising de Tocqueville did not figure in the early draft, and again it needs fascinating detailed exegesis to explain why. There was a long gap in Mill's correspondence with de Tocqueville between 1844 and 1856, probably because, for all their earlier mutual respect, they disagreed about de Tocqueville's views on the beneficent effects, in France at least, of militant nationalism. On Comte Mill is more candid, and the passages on the Saint-Simonians are much the same in the early and the final drafts.

From French writers Mill turns to the Englishmen who influenced his early life, particularly the members of the Utilitarian circle who looked to Bentham for their inspiration. Mill shows, however, that while they were undoubtedly Benthamites, they drew deeply on eighteenth-century philosophy, stated Benthamite tenets in language which was sometimes quite different in style and tone from Bentham's own, and shared many nineteenth-century opinions which derived from sources other than Bentham. "Malthus' population principle was quite as much a banner, and point of union among us, as any opinion specially belonging to Bentham." Mill used the name "Utilitarian" in the title of a little society of young men which he founded in 1822 at just about the time when he would have been starting his career as an undergraduate if his father had not disposed of his education for him. The fact that he did not have a university education is almost as important in understanding his career as the fact that he was taught no religion.

At a time when his contemporaries were undergraduates Mill was already a fully fledged intellectual, and Chapter IV of the *Autobiography* describes, often vividly, the way Benthamites argued with each other and with non-Benthamites and the way they set out to diffuse their opinions. "Representative government" and "complete freedom of discussion" were their watchwords. "The French *philosophes* of the eighteenth century were the example we sought to imitate, and we hoped to accomplish no less results." Far less has been written about the 1820's in English history than the years of Mill's maturity. For the mood of the period Mill is a main source. So too is the *Westminster Review,* the founding of which Mill describes. The debates of this period were the prelude to the Reforms of the 1830's. John Stuart Mill was entirely at one with the opinion expressed by his father in the first number of the *Westminster Review:* "The most effectual mode of doing good to mankind by reading is to correct their errors; to expose their prejudices; to refute opinions which are generated only by partial interests, but to which men are, for that reason, so much the more attached."

Mill gives a clearer picture in this chapter of his own mental development than he does of the character and outlook of people who were close to him. J. A. Roebuck, for example, was a Radical with a fascinating political career before him; in Mill's pages he scarcely comes to life. Grote, the Utilitarian historian of Greece, is a shadowy figure in the *Autobiography*, although as a result of his education Mill was always interested in Greek history. W. J. Fox, preacher, politician, and writer, is not mentioned at all in the context of the 1820's. Yet, in a strategic passage about the role of the Debating Society in 1825, Mill notes of himself: "I have always dated from these conversations my own real inauguration as an original and independent thinker. It was also through them that I acquired, or very much strengthened, a mental habit to which I attribute all that I have ever done, or ever shall do, in speculation: that of never accepting half-solutions of difficulties as complete; never abandoning a puzzle, but again and again returning to it until it was cleared up; never allowing obscure corners of a subject to remain unexplored because they did not appear important; never thinking that I perfectly understood any part of a subject until I understood the whole." Already Mill was anxious not only to explore particular branches of knowledge but to relate branches of knowledge which were later to become highly specialized; already, too, he was as interested in action as in argument, or rather in the driving force of argument as a means of motivating and rationalizing action. In one of the speeches which he delivered at the Debating Society in 1825 he ended with the peroration, "Knowledge has triumphed. It has worked the downfall of much that is mischievous. It is vain to suppose that it will pass by and spare any institution the existence of which is pernicious to mankind." This was a peroration which Mill might have delivered at any moment of his life.

Not only had Mill passed from reading to writing before many of his contemporaries had finished their formal education. He had also taken up the post, in 1823, which permitted him for thirty-five years to devote an exceptionally large amount of his time to writing. At the age of seventeen he obtained a clerkship in India House, the headquarters of the East India Company, where his father was an important official. He worked there until 1858, when the East India Company was disbanded. Few jobs could have left him so much time and independence to think and to expound. It is not surprising that he managed the resistance to the East India Company's extinction—he says little about *how* he managed it—and believed passionately that it was an act of "folly and mischief" to convert the administration of India into "a thing to be scrambled for by the second and third class of English parliamentary politicians." It is curious to think of the *Autobiography* and many of Mill's other writings as a by-product of East India Company rule in India.

By 1858, of course, Mill was well known to a large number of his fellow countrymen. In 1826, however, when he began his "crisis" he was simply a precocious young man of promise, a "youthful propagandist" with a half-formed intention of writing a history of the French Revolution. His "crisis" came at a time when he seemed, on the surface, to be increasingly settled both in his work and in his leisure. The most frightening aspect of his troubles, indeed, was that he began to doubt not only his early achievements but all his early ambitions. The whole foundation on which his life had been based, he complained, began to fall down. When he asked himself gloomily whether he would be happy even if all the objects he most desired in life were accomplished, he felt bound to answer no. Yet in the course of the "crisis," as he re-examined critically the Benthamite philosophies which his father had never doubted, he began to think more and more for himself, and, equally significant, to feel for himself. The "crisis" thus represented both a revolution in his "modes of thinking," the one revolution of this order in his life, and a re-evaluation of his need to cultivate his feelings and emotions.

At first the clouds grew thicker and thicker. Then he began to interest himself more and more in the consoling power of poetry and music. "The habit of analysis," he began to realize, "has a tendency to wear away the feelings." Wordsworth's poems, by contrast, were "a source of inward joy." Later Mill turned to Coleridge, Goethe, and Carlyle. For some time, indeed, Carlyle fulfilled Mill's need for a person to place on a pedestal, "a pedestal erected in Mill's soul," as Mrs. Borchard, one of his biographers suggests, "during his impressionable childhood." "I felt that he [Carlyle] was a poet," Mill wrote in the *Autobiography,* "and that I was not; that he was a man of intuition, which I was not; and that as such, he not only saw many things long before me . . . but that it was highly probable he could see many things which were not visible to me even after they were pointed out."

As a result of the crisis Mill felt that he had moved "one stage onward," that he was never the same again. He may well have exaggerated the newness of some of his thinking during and after the crisis, but he went on to pivot the whole interpretation of his intellectual life on what had happened in 1826. Because of this interpretation, nearly every writer on Mill has been forced to try to explain what really happened. Bain, his first biographer, thought that the crisis was physical: Mill had been "overworking the brain." Other biographers have turned to psychoanalysis. Mill himself admitted that his experience was far from unique, and compared his state of mind at the beginning of the crisis with that "in which converts to Methodism usually are, when smitten by their first conviction of sin."

Whatever the explanation of the crisis—and it is agreed by all biographers that it marked a reaction against his upbringing—it had general as well as particular implications. Mill's discovery of the inadequacy of doctrinaire Benthamism was one expression of a nineteenth-century revolt against the eighteenth century. His new "manysidedness," as he called it, his "willingness and ability to learn from everybody," prepared the way for the more eclectic form of utilitarianism which Mill was to expound in his later writings. The new mood was well expressed in a series of articles called "The Spirit of the Age," which he began in 1831. His essays on Bentham and Coleridge, written in 1838 and 1840 respectively, were essays of reconciliation, attempts to show that opinions which at first sight looked diametrically opposed to each other contained complementary truths. Both Bentham and Coleridge were "seminal minds." "To Bentham it was given to

discern more particularly those truths with which existing
doctrines and institutions were at variance; to Coleridge,
the neglected truths which lay *in* them."

As Mill read more widely and pondered on "the collision of opinions," which he welcomed as the only means
of reaching the truth, he converted a theory based on
individualism into a theory based on individuality, a theory
which treated happiness in quantitative terms as the object
of striving into a theory of qualitative happiness, in which
this end was only to be attained by not making it the direct
end. He "ceased to attach almost exclusive importance to
the ordering of outward circumstances," and laid greater
and greater stress on "the internal culture of the individual." John Bowring, the first editor of the *Westminster
Review* complained in 1840 that while Mill was "most
emphatically a philosopher," "he read Wordsworth and
that muddled him, and he has been in a strange confusion
ever since." Mill himself saw the story in terms of increasing wisdom: "Poetry is higher than logic, and . . . the
union of the two is philosophy."

While he continued to maintain that "happiness is the
test of all the rules of conduct, and the end of life," he
also maintained in his essay on Bentham that "a philosophy like Bentham's . . . can teach the means of organizing
and regulating the merely *business* part of the social arrangements . . . It will do nothing (except sometimes as an
instrument in the hands of a higher doctrine) for the
spiritual interests of society." Mill did not consider, as
some later writers were to do, that his "enlarged Benthamism" destroyed Bentham's intellectual foundations;
he rather saw it as more profound and apposite version of
a philosophy which needed to be modified in its expression
to suit different "states of the national mind."

As Mill became less sectarian, Carlyle soon ceased to
satisfy him. Towards the end of Chapter V of the *Autobiography* we learn of the intervention in Mill's life of
"one greatly the superior of us both—who was more a
poet than he, and more a thinker than I—whose own
mind and nature included his, and infinitely more." This
superior being was Harriet Taylor, whom Mill first met
in the summer or autumn of 1830, after she had been married for four years to John Taylor, eleven years her senior.
Mill was then twenty-five and Harriet twenty-three. Mill

described Taylor as "a most upright, brave, and honourable man ... but without the intellectual or artistic tastes which would have made him a companion" for his wife. Within a few years Mill's friendship with Harriet had ripened, and two years after Taylor's death in 1849 they married. By then he was convinced that the two of them constituted a very special kind of intellectual partnership, and that his writings were "not the work of one mind, but of the fusion of two."

The first part of Chapter VI of the *Autobiography* is devoted to "the commencement of the most valuable friendship of my life," and Harriet is described at the outset as "the honour and chief blessing of my existence." There are frequent references to the influence she had exerted on Mill's thinking and writing. Her mind was a "perfect instrument, piercing to the very heart and marrow of the matter." "What I owe, even intellectually, to her, is in its detail, almost infinite." Yet in his own account Mill admitted that her influence was brought to bear upon him only gradually. Whereas the "crisis" had been sudden and revolutionary, meeting and getting to know Harriet was gradual. The encounter between them "did not alter the path, but only made me move forward more boldly, and, at the same time, more cautiously in the same course."

What Mill says about Harriet in the *Autobiography* must be treated as a one-sided introduction to the subject of his relationship with her rather than as an account of it. The many tributes which he paid to her both in the *Autobiography* and in his other writings, notably in his preface to *On Liberty* and the reprint of an article on "The Enfranchisement of Women" in *Dissertations and Discussions,* demand the most careful critical scrutiny. Mill himself was concerned about what he could and could not reveal about their relationship. "We have to consider, which we can only do together," he told Harriet in 1854, "how much of our story it is advisable to tell, in order to make head against the representation of enemies when we shall not be alive to add anything to it. If it was not to be published for 100 years I should say, tell all, simply & without reserve. As it is there must be care taken not to put arms into the hands of the enemy."

Harriet read and corrected the early draft of the *Auto-*

biography, proposing many cuts and encouraging throughout Mill's effort to make it more of a public and less of a private document. There is no evidence, however, that she exercised even a fraction of the intellectual influence on Mill which he claimed. A detailed study of her reputed influence on specific works, such as the essay *On Liberty, The Subjection of Women,* or the famous chapter on "The Futurity of the Labouring Classes" in *Political Economy,* suggests that what Mill described as a central influence was at best peripheral or reinforcing. Bain rightly noted in 1882 that Mill "outraged all reasonable credulity in describing her [Harriet's] matchless genius, without being able to supply any corroborating testimony." Mill's brother George, who, like the rest of the Mill's family, became estranged after the marriage, said simply that she was "a clever and remarkable woman, but nothing like what John took her to be."

In the light of Mill's own comments and those of his friends, Harriet is perhaps best seen in the same context of emotional deprivation which made Mill turn for a time to Carlyle and earlier still to John Sterling, to whom he was "more attached . . . than I have ever been to any other man." Sterling was a Coleridgian, and Mill's response to Coleridge owed much to Sterling's mediation. "He and I started from intellectual points almost as wide apart as the poles, but the distance between us was always diminishing . . ." As one of Mill's biographers, Mrs. Borchard, has written, Mill always needed someone to be his "guiding star," man or woman. Harriet fulfilled this role so successfully and for such a long period that Mill saw her influence on his life as the culminating point of the *Autobiography* as he first conceived it. First came his education, with his father dominant; then his intellectual initiation, with Sterling, "one of the most lovable of men" as his first real friend; then the "crisis" which turned him towards Carlyle; and then, and last, the relationship with Harriet, the climax of his development. Already by 1833, before he had seen much of Harriet's intellectual work to which he was to acknowledge such an exaggerated debt, he wrote, "For me, I am certain that *whatever* she decides will be wisest and rightest."

At each stage in his mental development, therefore, Mill saw experience bringing with it new insights and new sensibilities. Feeling and thinking were very closely associated. "At a very early period of my knowledge of her," he wrote in the first draft of his *Autobiography*," she became to me a living type of the most admirable kind of human being. I had always wished for a friend whom I could admire wholly, without reservation and without restriction, and now I found one." The early draft ends, indeed, with their marriage, "the last considerable event in my own life." Her death in 1858 produced a reaction not unlike that of Queen Victoria after the death of Prince Albert in 1861, though Mill would have strongly disliked the parallel. "Her memory is to me a religion, and her approbation the standard by which, summing up as it does all worthiness, I endeavour to regulate my life." In the last years of his life, living in France, Mill transferred his affections to Harriet's daughter, Helen, "the inheritor of much of her [Harriet's] wisdom, and of all her nobleness of character, whose ever growing and ripening talents from that day to this have been devoted to the same great purposes."

Mill's estimate of Helen was so manifestly exaggerated —he even talked of three minds being responsible for his work, his own the "least original" of the three—that Bain persuaded Helen Taylor to leave out of the published draft of the *Autobiography* in 1873 certain passages which stretched credulity beyond all limits. The asterisks in the 1873 edition mark these places. Yet what remains amongst the rows of asterisks is revealing. "Surely no one ever before was so fortunate," Mill claimed, "as, after such a loss as mine, to draw another prize in the lottery of life."

There are three aspects of Mill's later life which are touched upon, but not fully explored, in the last sections of the *Autobiography*: first, his gradual move towards his own brand of "socialism"; second, his increasing emphasis on the need for encouraging "individuality"; and third, his parliamentary career. In 1865 he became a member of Parliament for Westminster, and sat in the House of Commons until his defeat at the next general election in 1868. He was thus a member of Parliament at the time of the debates on the second Reform Bill of 1867, when Disraeli's original proposals for a substantial measure of parliamentary reform were pushed far further than he had intended by Radical members of the opposition. Mill

was not a very interesting parliamentarian, however, for
he was determined "in general" to reserve himself "for
work which no others were likely to do." The canvassing
of opinions was what concerned him most, not the use
of power. He spoke in the House in favour of the abolition of capital punishment, the extension of the suffrage to
women, and the reform of London government. On the
last of these issues much of what he said anticipated
Fabian socialist writing of the 1890's.

Just because he was unconcerned with cutting a figure
in national politics, Mill's moves towards "socialism" in his
thinking are more interesting to the historian than his
parliamentary speeches or even his writings on the nature
of representative government. Mill had never believed in a
negative version of Benthamite utilitarianism, of the kind
which dogmatically repudiated state intervention. He
favoured state action to secure "the greatest happiness of
the greatest number" in such fields as education, poor
law, and public works. He was also a supporter of state
aid to research and of compulsory limitation of the hours
of work. Yet he never went as far as Edwin Chadwick,
the great Benthamite administrative reformer, who wanted
to use public power forcefully and unhesitantly, even if it
meant overriding "public opinion." Mill believed too much
in public opinion to interpret its influence in terms of the
clamour of vested interests or the ignorance of people who
would not listen to sound advice. He had no hankering
after Chadwick's "administrative state." He came to believe, however, that "the social problem of the future"
was "how to unite the greatest individual liberty of action
with a common ownership in the raw material of the globe,
and an equal participation of all in the benefits of combined
labour." In seeking to wrestle with this problem, society
would have to pay increasing attention to education: ". . .
to render any such social transformation either possible or
desirable, an equivalent change of character must take
place both in the uncultivated herd who now compose the
labouring masses, and in the immense majority of their
employers."

In the few passages in the *Autobiography* which deal
with issues of this kind, Mill sometimes seems closer to
Matthew Arnold than he is on any other occasion. He also
emerges as a resolute critic of an economic and social

order exclusively concerned with the pursuit of self-interest. His belief in "individuality" was not incompatible with his demand for "socialism." Indeed, he anticipated late-Victorian writers who argued, as Oscar Wilde was to do in *The Soul of Man under Socialism*, that true individuality could best be achieved within a socialist system. In his late thought, as in his early thought, however, Mill continued to stress the necessity for an intellectual revolution as a pre-condition of all other kinds of change. "I am now convinced," he wrote in the *Autobiography*, "that no great improvements in the lot of mankind are possible until a great change takes place in the fundamental constitution of their modes of thought." Such an approach made him a popular figure among the late-Victorian rebels, a more popular figure than many of his contemporaries, who, by comparison, seemed to be both inhibited and dated. It was in 1890 that Helen Taylor remarked happily that so many reform movements were flourishing in England that she felt herself to be living in one of the great ages—an age when a remarkable quickening of conscience was taking place.

Mill's *Autobiography* takes its place with the many great Victorian books which chart the way to the modern world. It will remain of profound importance, however, not only to students of Benthamism or Fabianism or of the links between them, but to students of the relationship between psychology and sociology: thought and feeling on the one hand and will and action on the other. While James Mill was busy educating his son, he wrote to Francis Place, the London Radical tailor, who was also engaged in educating a son, telling him "not to exact too great things from him." "That is the fault of all of us," he went on, "whose notions of perfection are high and aspirations after it keen." It is an engaging letter, for it continues, "This is a doctrine you have as much need to preach to me as I to you." Whatever the deficiencies of John Stuart Mill's education, it produced John Stuart Mill. Whatever the deficiencies of Benthamism, it set Mill on a way of thinking which was both practical and creative. Whatever the intellectual capabilities of Harriet, she made Mill happier and more secure than he might otherwise have been. As Dr. Pappé has written in the most perceptive of the many studies of their relationship, "her cooperation with Mill was, in difficult circumstances, an early example of that husband-wife partnership which, thanks to the efforts of people like the Mills, has blissfully become more frequent in our time."

ASA BRIGGS
UNIVERSITY OF SUSSEX

autobiography of
JOHN STUART MILLS

CHILDHOOD AND EARLY EDUCATION

It seems proper that I should prefix to the following biographical sketch some mention of the reasons which have made me think it desirable that I should leave behind me such a memorial of so uneventful a life as mine. I do not for a moment imagine that any part of what I have to relate can be interesting to the public as a narrative, or as being connected with myself. But I have thought that in an age in which education, and its improvement, are the subject of more, if not of profounder study than at any former period of English history, it may be useful that there should be some record of an education which was unusual and remarkable, and which, whatever else it may have done, has proved how much more than is commonly supposed may be taught, and well taught, in those early years which, in the common modes of what is called instruction, are little better than wasted. It has also seemed to me that in an age of transition in opinions, there may be somewhat both of interest and of benefit in noting the successive phases of any mind which was always pressing forward, equally ready to learn and to un-learn either from its own thoughts or from those of others. But a motive which weighs more with me than either of these is a desire to make acknowledgement of the debts which my intellectual and moral development owes to other persons; some of them of recognized eminence, others less known than they deserve to be, and the one to whom most of all is due, one whom the world had no opportunity of knowing. The reader whom these things do not interest has only himself to blame if he reads farther, and I do not desire any other indulgence from him than that of bearing in mind that for him these pages were not written.

I was born in London, on the 20th of May, 1806, and was the eldest son of James Mill, the author of the *History of British India*. My father, the son of a petty tradesman and (I believe) small farmer, at Northwater Bridge, in the county of Angus, was, when a boy, recom-mended by his abilities to the notice of Sir John Stuart, of Fettercairn, one of the Barons of the Exchequer in Scotland, and was, in consequence, sent to the University of Edinburgh, at the expense of a fund established by Lady Jane Stuart (the wife of Sir John Stuart) and some other ladies for educating young men for the Scottish Church. He there went through the usual course of study, and was licensed as a preacher, but never followed the profession; having satisfied himself that he could not be-lieve the doctrines of that or any other Church. For a few years he was a private tutor in various families in Scot-land, among others that of the Marquis of Tweeddale, but ended by taking up his residence in London, and devoting himself to authorship. Nor had he any other means of support until 1819, when he obtained an appointment in the India House.

In this period of my father's life there are two things which it is impossible not to be struck with: one of them unfortunately a very common circumstance, the other a most uncommon one. The first is that in his position, with no resource but the precarious one of writing in periodicals, he married and had a large family; conduct than which nothing could be more opposed, both as a matter of good sense and of duty, to the opinions which, at least at a later period of life, he strenuously upheld. The other circumstance is the extraordinary energy which was required to lead the life he led, with the disadvantages under which he laboured from the first, and with those which he brought upon himself by his marriage. It would have been no small thing had he done no more than to support himself and his family during so many years by writing, without ever being in debt, or in any pecuniary difficulty; holding, as he did, opinions, both in politics and in religion, which were more odious to all persons of influence, and to the common run of prosperous Englishmen in that generation than either before or since; and being not only a man whom nothing would have induced to write against his convictions, but one who invariably threw into everything he wrote as much of his convictions as he thought the circumstances would in any way permit: being, it must also be said, one who never did anything negligently; never undertook any task, literary or other, on which he did not conscientiously bestow all the labour necessary for performing it adequately. But he, with these burdens on him, planned, commenced, and completed, the *History of India*; and this in the course of about ten years, a shorter time than has been occupied (even by writers who had no other employment) in the production of almost any other historical work of equal bulk, and of anything approaching to the same amount of reading and research. And to this is to be added that during the whole period a considerable part of almost every day was employed in the instruction of his children: in the case of one of whom, myself, he exerted an amount of labour, care and perseverance rarely, if ever, employed for a similar purpose, in endeavouring to give, according to his own conception, the highest order of intellectual education.

A man who, in his own practice, so vigorously acted up to the principle of losing no time was likely to adhere to the same rule in the instruction of his pupil. I have no remembrance of the time when I began to learn Greek; I have been told that it was when I was three years old. My earliest recollection on the subject is that of committing to memory what my father termed vocables, being lists of common Greek words, with their signification in English, which he wrote out for me on cards. Of grammar, until some years later, I learnt no more than the inflexions of the nouns and verbs, but, after a course of vocables, proceeded at once to translation; and I faintly remember going through *Aesop's Fables*, the first Greek book which I read. The *Anabasis*, which I remember better, was the second. I learnt no Latin until my eighth year. At that time I had read, under my father's tuition, a number of Greek prose authors, among whom I remember the whole of Herodotus, and of Xenophon's *Cyropaedia* and memorials of Socrates; some of the lives of the philosophers by Diogenes Laërtius; part of Lucian, and Isocrates *Ad Demonicum* and *Ad Nicoclem*. I also read, in 1813, the first six dialogues (in the common arrangement) of Plato, from the *Euthyphron* to the *Theaetetus* inclusive; which last dialogue, I venture to think, would have been better omitted, as it was totally impossible I should understand it. But my father, in all his teaching, demanded of me not only the utmost that I could do, but much that I could by no possibility have done. What he was himself willing to undergo for the sake of my instruction may be judged from the fact that I went through the whole process of preparing my Greek lessons in the same room and at the same table at which he was writing; and as in those days Greek and English lexicons were not, and I could make no more use of a Greek and Latin lexicon than could be made without having yet begun to learn Latin, I was forced to have recourse to him for the meaning of every word which I did not know. This incessant interruption, he, one of the most impatient of men, submitted to, and wrote under that interruption several volumes of his *History* and all else that he had to write during those years.

The only thing besides Greek that I learnt as a lesson, in this part of my childhood, was arithmetic; this also my father taught me—it was the task of the evenings, and I well remember its disagreeableness. But the lessons were only a part of the daily instruction I received. Much of it consisted in the books I read by myself, and my father's discourses to me, chiefly during our walks. From 1810 to the end of 1813 we were living in Newington Green, then an almost rustic neighbourhood. My father's health required considerable and constant exercise, and he walked habitually before breakfast, generally in the green lanes towards Hornsey. In these walks I always accompanied him, and with my earliest recollections of green fields and wild flowers is mingled that of the account I gave him daily of what I had read the day before. To the best of my remembrance this was voluntary rather than a prescribed exercise. I made notes on slips of paper while reading, and from these, in the morning walks, I told the story to him; for the books were chiefly histories, of which I read in this manner a great number: Robertson's histories, Hume, Gibbon; but my greatest delight, then and for long afterwards, was Watson's *Philip the Second and Third*. The heroic defence of the Knights of Malta against the Turks, and of the revolted Provinces of the Netherlands against Spain, excited in me an intense and lasting interest. Next to Watson, my favourite historical reading was Hooke's *History of Rome*. Of Greece I had seen at that time no regular history, except school abridgements and the last two or three volumes of a translation of Rollin's *Ancient History*, beginning with Philip of Macedon. But I read with great delight Langhorne's translation of Plutarch. In English history, beyond the time at which Hume leaves off, I remember reading Burnet's *History of My Own Time*, though I cared little for anything in it except the wars and battles; and the historical part of the *Annual Register*, from the beginning to about 1788, where the volumes my father borrowed for me from Mr. Bentham left off. I felt a lively interest in Frederick of Prussia during his difficulties, and in Paoli, the Corsican patriot; but when I came to the American war, I took my part, like a child as I was (until set right by my father) on the wrong side, because it was called the English side. In these frequent talks about the books I read, he used, as opportunity offered, to give me explanations and ideas respecting civilization, government, morality, mental cultivation, which he required me afterwards to restate to him in my own words. He also made me read, and give him a verbal account of, many books which would not have interested me sufficiently to induce me to read them of myself: among others, Millar's *Historical View of the English Government*, a book of great merit for its time, and which he highly valued; Mosheim's *Ecclesiastical History*, McCrie's *Life of John Knox*, and even Sewell and Rutty's *Histories of the Quakers*. He was fond of putting into my hands books which exhibited men of

energy and resource in unusual circumstances, struggling
against difficulties and overcoming them: of such works
I remember Beaver's *African Memoranda,* and Collins'
Account of the First Settlement of New South Wales. Two
books which I never wearied of reading were Anson's
Voyages, so delightful to most young persons, and a collection (Hawkesworth's, I believe) of *Voyages Round the
World,* in four volumes, beginning with Drake and ending
with Cook and Bougainville. Of children's books, any
more than of playthings, I had scarcely any, except an occasional gift from a relation or acquaintance: among those
I had, Robinson Crusoe was pre-eminent, and continued
to delight me through all my boyhood. It was no part,
however, of my father's system to exclude books of amusement, though he allowed them very sparingly. Of such
books he possessed at that time next to none, but he borrowed several for me; those which I remember are the
Arabian Nights, Cazotte's *Arabian Tales, Don Quixote,*
Miss Edgewood's *Popular Tales,* and a book of some reputation in its day, Brooke's *Fool of Quality.*

In my eighth year I commenced learning Latin, in conjunction with a younger sister, to whom I taught it as I
went on, and who afterwards repeated the lessons to my
father; and from this time, other sisters and brothers being
successively added as pupils, a considerable part of my
day's work consisted of this preparatory teaching. It was
a part which I greatly disliked; the more so as I was held
responsible for the lessons of my pupils in almost as full a
sense as for my own; I, however, derived from this discipline the great advantage of learning more thoroughly
and retaining more lastingly the things which I was set
to teach; perhaps, too, the practice it afforded in explaining difficulties to others may even at that age have been
useful. In other respects, the experience of my boyhood
is not favourable to the plan of teaching children by means
of one another. The teaching, I am sure, is very inefficient
as teaching, and I well know that the relation between
teacher and taught is not a good moral discipline to either.
I went in this manner through the Latin grammar, and a
considerable part of Cornelius Nepos and Caesar's *Com-
mentaries,* but afterwards added to the superintendence of
these lessons much longer ones of my own.

In the same year in which I began Latin, I made

my first commencement in the Greek poets with the *Iliad*. After I had made some progress in this, my father put Pope's translation into my hands. It was the first English verse I had cared to read, and it became one of the books in which for many years I most delighted: I think I must have read it from twenty to thirty times through. I should not have thought it worth-while to mention a taste apparently so natural to boyhood if I had not, as I think, observed that the keen enjoyment of this brilliant specimen of narrative and versification is not so universal with boys as I should have expected both a priori and from my individual experience. Soon after this time I commenced Euclid, and somewhat later, algebra, still under my father's tuition.

From my eighth to my twelfth year, the Latin books which I remember reading were the *Bucolics* of Virgil, and the first six books of the *Aeneid*; all Horace, except the *Epodes*; the *Fables* of Phaedrus; the first five books of Livy (to which from my love of the subject I voluntarily added, in my hours of leisure, the remainder of the first decade); all Sallust; a considerable part of Ovid's *Metamorphoses;* some plays of Terence; two or three books of Lucretius; several of the orations of Cicero, and of his writings on oratory; also his letters to Atticus, my father taking the trouble to translate to me from the French the historical explanations in Mingault's notes. In Greek I read the *Iliad* and *Odyssey* through; one or two plays of Sophocles, Euripides, and Aristophanes, though by these I profited little; all Thucydides; the *Hellenics* of Xenophon; a great part of Demosthenes, Aeschines, and Lysias; Theocritus; Anacreon; part of the *Anthology*; a little of Dionysius; several books of Polybius; and lastly Aristotle's *Rhetoric,* which, as the first expressly scientific treatise on any moral or psychological subject which I had read, and containing many of the best observations of the ancients on human nature and life, my father made me study with peculiar care, and throw the matter of it into synoptic tables. During the same years I learnt elementary geometry and algebra thoroughly, the differential calculus, and other portions of the higher mathematics far from thoroughly; for my father, not having kept up this part of his early acquired knowledge, could not spare time to qualify himself for removing my difficulties, and left me

to deal with them, with little other aid than that of books
—while I was continually incurring his displeasure by my
inability to solve difficult problems for which he did not
see that I had not the necessary previous knowledge.

As to my private reading, I can only speak of what
I remember. History continued to be my strongest pre-
dilection, and most of all ancient history. Mitford's *Greece*
I read continually; my father had put me on my guard
against the Tory prejudices of this writer, and his perver-
sions of facts for the whitewashing of despots, and black-
ening of popular institutions. These points he discoursed
on, exemplifying them from the Greek orators and his-
torians, with such effect that in reading Mitford my sympathies were always on the contrary side to those of the
author, and I could, to some extent, have argued the
point against him; yet this did not diminish the ever new
pleasure with which I read the book. Roman history,
both in my old favourite, Hooke, and in Ferguson, continued to delight me. A book which, in spite of what is
called the dryness of its style, I took great pleasure in,
was the *Ancient Universal History,* through the incessant
reading of which I had my head full of historical details
concerning the obscurest ancient people, while about modern history, except detached passages, such as the Dutch
War of Independence, I knew and cared comparatively
little. A voluntary exercise, to which throughout my boyhood I was much addicted, was what I called writing histories. I successively composed a "Roman History", picked
out of Hooke; an "Abridgment of the Ancient Universal
History"; a "History of Holland," from my favourite Watson and from an anonymous compilation; and in my
eleventh and twelfth year I occupied myself with writing
what I flattered myself was something serious. This was
no less than a "History of the Roman Government," com-
piled (with the assistance of Hooke) from Livy and Dionysius; of which I wrote as much as would have made an
octavo volume, extending to the epoch of the Licinian
Laws. It was, in fact, an account of the struggles between
the patricians and plebeians which now engrossed all the
interest in my mind which I had previously felt in the
mere wars and conquests of the Romans. I discussed all
the constitutional points as they arose: though quite ignorant of Niebuhr's researches, I, by such lights as my father

had given me, vindicated the Agrarian Laws on the evidence of Livy, and upheld, to the best of my ability, the Roman Democratic party. A few years later, in my contempt of my childish efforts, I destroyed all these papers, not then anticipating that I could ever feel any curiosity about my first attempts at writing and reasoning. My father encouraged me in this useful amusement, though, as I think judiciously, he never asked to see what I wrote; so that I did not feel that in writing it I was accountable to any one, nor had the chilling sensation of being under a critical eye.

But though these exercises in history were never a compulsory lesson, there was another kind of composition which was so, namely, writing verses, and it was one of the most disagreeable of my tasks. Greek and Latin verses I did not write, nor learnt the prosody of those languages. My father, thinking this not worth the time it required, contented himself with making me read aloud to him, and correcting false quantities. I never composed at all in Greek, even in prose, and but little in Latin. Not that my father could be indifferent to the value of this practice in giving a thorough knowledge of these languages, but because there really was not time for it. The verses I was required to write were English. When I first read Pope's Homer, I ambitiously attemped to compose something of the same kind, and achieved as much as one book of a continuation of the *Iliad*. There, probably, the spontaneous promptings of my poetical ambition would have stopped; but the exercise, begun from choice, was continued by command. Conformably to my father's usual practice of explaining to me, as far as possible, the reasons for what he required me to do, he gave me, for this, as I well remember, two reasons highly characteristic of him: one was, that some things could be expressed better and more forcibly in verse than in prose; this, he said, was a real advantage. The other was, that people in general attached more value to verse than it deserved, and the power of writing it, was, on this account, worth acquiring. He generally left me to choose my own subjects, which, as far as I remember, were mostly addresses to some mythological personage or allegorical abstraction; but he made me translate into English verse many of Horace's shorter poems; I also remember his giving me Thomson's

"Winter" to read, and afterwards making me attempt (without book) to write something myself on the same subject. The verses I wrote were, of course, the merest rubbish, nor did I ever attain any facility of versification, but the practice may have been useful in making it easier for me, at a later period, to acquire readiness of expression.* I had read, up to this time, very little English poetry. Shakspeare my father had put into my hands chiefly for the sake of the historical plays, from which, however, I went on to the others. My father never was a great admirer of Shakspeare, the English idolatry of whom he used to attack with some severity. He cared little for any English poetry except Milton (for whom he had the highest admiration), Goldsmith, Burns, and Gray's *Bard,* which he preferred to his *Elegy;* perhaps I may add Cowper and Beattie. He had some value for Spenser, and I remember his reading to me (unlike his usual practice of making me read to him), the first book of the *Faerie Queene;* but I took little pleasure in it. The poetry of the present century he saw scarcely any merit in, and I hardly became acquainted with any of it till I was grown up to manhood, except the metrical romances of Walter Scott, which I read at his recommendation and was intensely delighted with; as I always was with animated narrative. Dryden's *Poems* were among my father's books, and many of these he made me read, but I never cared for any of them except "Alexander's Feast," which, as well as many of the songs in Walter Scott, I used to sing internally, to a music of my own; to some of the latter, indeed, I went so far as to compose airs, which I still remember. Cowper's short poems I read with some pleasure, but never got far into the longer ones; and nothing in the two volumes interested me like the prose account of his three hares. In my thirteenth year I met with Campbell's poems, among which "Lochiel," "Hohenlinden," "The Exile of Erin," and some others, gave me sensations I had never before experienced from poetry. Here, too, I made nothing of the longer

* In a subsequent stage of boyhood, when these exercises had ceased to be compulsory, like most youthful writers I wrote tragedies; under the inspiration not so much of Shakspeare as of Joanna Baillie, whose *Constantine Paleologus* in particular appeared to me one of the most glorious of human compositions. I still think it one of the best dramas of the last two centuries.

poems, except the striking opening of "Gertrude of Wyo-
ming," which long kept its place in my feelings as the perfection of pathos.

During this part of my childhood, one of my greatest
amusements was experimental science; in the theoretical,
however, not the practical sense of the word; not trying
experiments—a kind of discipline which I have often
regretted not having had—nor even seeing, but merely
reading about them. I never remember being so wrapped
up in any book as I was in Joyce's *Scientific Dialogues;*
and I was rather recalcitrant to my father's criticisms of
the bad reasoning respecting the first principles of physics,
which abounds in the early part of that work. I devoured
treatises on chemistry, especially that of my father's early
friend and schoolfellow, Dr. Thomson, for years before
I attended a lecture or saw an experiment.

From about the age of twelve, I entered into another
and more advanced stage in my course of instruction; in
which the main object was no longer the aids and ap-
pliances of thought, but the thoughts themselves. This
commenced with logic, in which I began at once with the
Organon, and read it to the *Analytics* inclusive, but profited little by the *Posterior Analytics,* which belong to a
branch of speculation I was not yet ripe for. Contempora-
neously with the *Organon,* my father made me read the
whole or parts of several of the Latin treatises on the
scholastic logic; giving each day to him, in our walks, a
minute account of what I had read, and answering his
numerous and searching questions. After this, I went in a
similar manner, through the *Computatio sive Logica* of
Hobbes, a work of a much higher order of thought than
the books of the school logicians, and which he estimated
very highly; in my own opinion beyond its merits, great
as these are. It was his invariable practice, whatever
studies he exacted from me, to make me as far as possible
understand and feel the utility of them; and this he deemed
peculiarly fitting in the case of the syllogistic logic, the
usefulness of which had been impugned by so many
writers of authority. I well remember how, and in what
particular walk, in the neighbourhood of Bagshot Heath
(where we were on a visit to his old friend Mr. Wallace,
then one of the Mathematical Professors at Sandhurst),
he first attempted by questions to make me think on the

subject, and frame some conception of what constituted the utility of the syllogistic logic, and, when I had failed in this, to make me understand it by explanations. The explanations did not make the matter at all clear to me at the time; but they were not therefore useless; they remained as a nucleus for my observations and reflections to crystallize upon; the import of his general remarks being interpreted to me by the particular instances which came under my notice afterwards. My own consciousness and experience ultimately led me to appreciate quite as highly as he did the value of an early practical familiarity with the school logic. I know of nothing, in my education, to which I think myself more indebted for whatever capacity of thinking I have attained. The first intellectual operation in which I arrived at any proficiency was dissecting a bad argument, and finding in what part the fallacy lay; and though whatever capacity of this sort I attained was due to the fact that it was an intellectual exercise in which I was most perseveringly drilled by my father, yet it is also true that the school logic, and the mental habits acquired in studying it, were among the principal instruments of this drilling. I am persuaded that nothing, in modern education, tends so much, when properly used, to form exact thinkers, who attach a precise meaning to words and propositions, and are not imposed on by vague, loose, or ambiguous terms. The boasted influence of mathematical studies is nothing to it; for in mathematical processes, none of the real difficulties of correct ratiocination occur. It is also a study peculiarly adapted to an early stage in the education of philosophical students, since it does not presuppose the slow process of acquiring, by experience and reflection, valuable thoughts of their own. They may become capable of disentangling the intricacies of confused and self-contradictory thought before their own thinking faculties are much advanced; a power which, for want of some such discipline, many otherwise able men altogether lack; and when they have to answer opponents, only endeavour, by such arguments as they can command, to support the opposite conclusion, scarcely even attempting to confute the reasonings of their antagonists; and, therefore, at the utmost, leaving the question, as far as it depends on argument, a balanced one.

During this time, the Latin and Greek books which I

continued to read with my father were chiefly such as
were worth studying, not for the language merely, but also
for the thoughts. This included much of the orators, and
especially Demosthenes, some of whose principal orations
I read several times over, and wrote out, by way of exercise, a full analysis of them. My father's comments on
these orations when I read them to him were very instructive to me. He not only drew my attention to the
insight they afforded into Athenian institutions, and the
principles of legislation and government which they often
illustrated, but pointed out the skill and art of the orator—
how everything important to his purpose was said at the
exact moment when he had brought the minds of his audience into the state most fitted to receive it; how he made
steal into their minds, gradually and by insinuation,
thoughts which, if expressed in a more direct manner,
would have roused their opposition. Most of these reflections were beyond my capacity of full comprehension at the
time; but they left seed behind, which germinated in due
season. At this time I also read the whole of Tacitus, Juve-
nal, and Quintilian. The latter, owing to his obscure style
and to the scholastic details of which many parts of his
treatise are made up, is little read, and seldom sufficiently
appreciated. His book is a kind of encyclopaedia of the
thoughts of the ancients on the whole field of education and
culture; and I have retained through life many valuable
ideas which I can distinctly trace to my reading of him,
even at that early age. It was at this period that I read, for
the first time, some of the most important dialogues of
Plato, in particular the *Gorgias*, the *Protagoras*, and the
Republic. There is no author to whom my father thought
himself more indebted for his own mental culture than
Plato, or whom he more frequently recommended to young
students. I can bear similar testimony in regard to myself.
The Socratic method, of which the Platonic dialogues are
the chief example, is unsurpassed as a discipline for correcting the errors, and clearing up the confusions incident
to the *intellectus sibi permissus,* the understanding which
has made up all its bundles of associations under the guidance of popular phraseology. The close, searching *elenchus*
by which the man of vague generalities is constrained either
to express his meaning to himself in definite terms, or to
confess that he does not know what he is talking about;

the perpetual testing of all general statements by particular instances; the siege in form which is laid to the meaning of large abstract terms, by fixing upon some still larger class-name which includes that and more, and dividing down to the thing sought—marking out its limits and definition by a series of accurately drawn distinctions between it and each of the cognate objects which are successively parted off from it—all this, as an education for precise thinking, is inestimable, and all this, even at that age, took such hold of me that it became part of my own mind. I have felt ever since that the title of Platonist belongs by far better right to those who have been nourished in, and have endeavoured to practise Plato's mode of investigation, than to those who are distinguished only by the adoption of certain dogmatical conclusions, drawn mostly from the least intelligible of his works, and which the character of his mind and writings makes it uncertain whether he himself regarded as anything more than poetic fancies, or philosophic conjectures.

In going through Plato and Demosthenes, since I could now read these authors, as far as the language was concerned, with perfect ease, I was not required to construe them sentence by sentence, but to read them aloud to my father, answering questions when asked; but the particular attention which he paid to elocution (in which his own excellence was remarkable) made this reading aloud to him a most painful task. Of all things which he required me to do, there was none which I did so constantly ill, or in which he so perpetually lost his temper with me. He had thought much on the principles of the art of reading, especially the most neglected part of it, the inflections of the voice, or *modulation* as writers on elocution call it (in contrast with *articulation* on the one side, and *expression* on the other), and had reduced it to rules, grounded on the logical analysis of a sentence. These rules he strongly impressed upon me, and took me severely to task for every violation of them; but I even then remarked (though I did not venture to make the remark to him) that though he reproached me when I read a sentence ill, and *told* me how I ought to have read it, he never, by reading it himself, *showed* me how it ought to be read. A defect running through his otherwise admirable modes of instruction, as it did through all his modes of thought, was that of trusting too much to the intelligibleness of the abstract, when not embodied in the concrete. It was at a much later period of my youth, when practising elocution by myself, or with companions of my own age, that I for the first time understood the object of his rules, and saw the psychological grounds of them. At that time I and others followed out the subject into its ramifications and could have composed a very useful treatise, grounded on my father's principles. He himself left those principles and rules unwritten. I regret that when my mind was full of the subject, from systematic practice, I did not put them, and our improvements of them, into a formal shape.

A book which contributed largely to my education, in the best sense of the term, was my father's *History of India*. It was published in the beginning of 1818. During the year previous, which it was passing through the press, I used to read the proof sheets to him; or rather, I read the manuscript to him while he corrected the proofs. The number of new ideas which I received from this remarkable book, and the impulse and stimulus as well as guidance given to my thoughts by its criticisms and disquisitions on society and civilization in the Hindu part, on institutions and the acts of governments in the English part, made my early familiarity with it eminently useful to my subsequent progress. And though I can perceive deficiencies in it now as compared with a perfect standard, I still think it, if not the most, one of the most instructive histories ever written, and one of the books from which most benefit may be derived by a mind in the course of making up its opinions.

The Preface, among the most characteristic of my father's writings, as well as the richest in materials of thought, gives a picture which may be entirely depended on, of the sentiments and expectations with which he wrote the *History*. Saturated as the book is with the opinions and modes of judgement of a democratic radicalism then regarded as extreme, and treating with a severity, at that time most unusual, the English Constitution, the English law, and all parties and classes who possessed any considerable influence in the country, he may have expected reputation, but certainly not advancement in life, from its publication; nor could he have supposed that it would raise up anything but enemies for him in powerful quarters: least of all could he have expected favour from the East India Company, to whose commercial privileges he was unqualifiedly hostile, and on the acts of whose government he had made so many severe comments—though, in various parts of his book, he bore a testimony in their favour, which he felt to be their just due, namely, that no government had on the whole given so much proof, to the extent of its lights, of good intention towards its subjects; and that if the acts of any other government had the light of publicity as completely let in upon them, they would, in all probability, still less bear scrutiny.

On learning, however, in the spring of 1819, about a year after the publication of the *History,* that the East India Directors desired to strengthen the part of their home establishment which was employed in carrying on the correspondence with India, my father declared himself a candidate for that employment, and, to the credit of the Directors, successfully. He was appointed one of the Assistants of the Examiner of India Correspondence; officers whose duty it was to prepare drafts of dispatches to India, for consideration by the Directors, in the principal departments of administration. In this office, and in that of Examiner, which he subsequently attained, the influence, which his talents, his reputation, and his decision of character gave him with superiors who really desired the good government of India, enabled him to a great extent to throw into his drafts of dispatches, and to carry through the ordeal of the Court of Directors and Board of Control, without having their force much weakened, his real opinions on Indian subjects. In his *History* he had set forth, for the first time, many of the true principles of Indian administration; and his dispatches, following his *History,* did more than had ever been done before to promote the improvement of India, and teach Indian officials to understand their business. If a selection of them were published, they would, I am convinced, place his character as a practical statesman fully on a level with his eminence as a speculative writer.

This new employment of his time caused no relaxation in his attention to my education. It was in this same year, 1819, that he took me through a complete course of political economy. His loved and intimate friend, Ricardo, had shortly before published the book which formed so great an epoch in political economy; a book which never would have been published or written, but for the entreaty and strong encouragement of my father; for Ricardo, the most modest of men, though firmly convinced of the truth of his doctrines, deemed himself so little capable of doing them justice in exposition and expression that he shrank from the idea of publicity. The same friendly encouragement induced Ricardo, a year or two later, to become a member of the House of Commons; where, during the few remaining years of his life, unhappily cut short in the full vigour of his intellect, he rendered so much service to his and my father's opinions both on political economy and on other subjects.

Though Ricardo's great work was already in print, no didactic treatise embodying its doctrines, in a manner fit for learners, had yet appeared. My father, therefore, commenced instructing me in the science by a sort of lectures, which he delivered to me in our walks. He expounded each day a portion of the subject, and I gave him next day a written account of it, which he made me rewrite over and over again until it was clear, precise, and tolerably complete. In this manner I went through the whole extent of the science; and the written outline of it, which resulted from my daily *compte rendu,* served him afterwards as notes from which to write his *Elements of Political Economy.* After this I read Ricardo, giving an account daily of what I read, and discussing, in the best manner I could, the collateral points which offered themselves in our progress.

On money, as the most intricate part of the subject, he made me read in the same manner Ricardo's admirable pamphlets, written during what was called the bullion controversy; to these succeeded Adam Smith; and in this reading it was one of my father's main objects to make me apply to Smith's more superficial view of political economy the superior lights of Ricardo, and detect what was fallacious in Smith's arguments, or erroneous in any of his conclusions. Such a mode of instruction was excellently calculated to form a thinker; but it required to be worked by a thinker as close and vigorous as my father. The path was a thorny one, even to him, and I am sure it was so to me, notwithstanding the strong interest I took in the subject. He was often, and much beyond reason, provoked by my failures in cases where success could not have been expected; but in the main his method was right, and it succeeded. I do not believe that any scientific teaching ever was more thorough, or better fitted for training the faculties, than the mode in which logic and political economy were taught to me by my father. Striving, even in an exaggerated degree, to call forth the activity of my faculties, by making me find out everything for myself, he gave his explanations not before, but after, I had felt the full force of the difficulties; and not only gave me an accurate knowledge of these two great subjects, as far as they were then understood, but made me a thinker on both. I thought for myself almost from the first, and occasionally thought differently from him, though for a long time only on minor points, and making his opinion the ultimate standard. At a later period I even occasionally convinced him, and altered his opinion on some points of detail: which I state to his honour, not my own. It at once exemplifies his perfect candour, and the real worth of his method of teaching.

At this point concluded what can properly be called my lessons: when I was about fourteen I left England for more than a year; and after my return, though my studies went on under my father's general direction, he was no longer my schoolmaster. I shall therefore pause here, and turn back to matters of a more general nature connected with the part of my life and education included in the preceding reminiscences.

In the course of instruction which I have partially re-traced, the point most superficially apparent is the great effort to give, during the years of childhood, an amount of knowledge in what are considered the higher branches of education, which is seldom acquired (if acquired at all) until the age of manhood. The result of the experiment shows the ease with which this may be done, and places in a strong light the wretched waste of so many precious years as are spent in acquiring the modicum of Latin and Greek commonly taught to schoolboys; a waste which has led so many educational reformers to entertain the ill-judged proposal of discarding these languages altogether from general education. If I had been by nature extremely quick of apprehension, or had possessed a very accurate and retentive memory, or were of a remarkably active and energetic character, the trial would not be conclusive; but in all these natural gifts I am rather below than above par; what I could do could assuredly be done by any boy or girl of average capacity and healthy physical constitution; and if I have accomplished anything, I owe it, among other fortunate circumstances, to the fact that through the early training bestowed on me by my father, I started, I may fairly say, with an advantage of a quarter of a century over my contemporaries.

There was one cardinal point in this training, of which I have already given some indication, and which, more than anything else, was the cause of whatever good it effected. Most boys or youths who have had much knowledge drilled into them have their mental capacities not strengthened, but overlaid by it. They are crammed with mere facts, and with the opinions or phrases of other people, and these are accepted as a substitute for the power to form opinions of their own; and thus the sons of eminent fathers, who have spared no pains in their education, so often grow up mere parroters of what they have learnt, incapable of using their minds except in the furrows traced for them. Mine, however, was not an education of cram. My father never permitted anything which I learnt to degenerate into a mere exercise of memory. He strove to make the understanding not only go along with every step of the teaching, but, if possible, precede it. Anything which could be found out by thinking I never was told until I had exhausted my efforts to find it out for myself. As far as I can trust my remembrance, I acquitted myself very lamely in this department; my recollection of such matters is almost wholly of failures, hardly ever of success. It is true the failures were often in things in which success in so early a stage of my progress was almost impossible. I remember at some time in my thirteenth year, on my happening to use the word idea, he asked me what an idea was; and expressed some displeasure at my ineffectual efforts to define the word; I recollect also his indignation at my using the common expression that sometimes was true in theory but required correction in practice; and how, after making me vainly strive to define the word theory, he explained its meaning, and showed the fallacy of the vulgar form of speech which I had used; leaving me fully persuaded that in being unable to give a correct definition of theory, and in speaking of it as something which might be at variance with practice, I had shown unparalleled ignorance. In this he seems, and perhaps was, very unreasonable; but I think, only in being angry at my failure. A pupil from whom nothing is ever demanded which he cannot do never does all he can.

One of the evils most liable to attend on any sort of early proficiency, and which often fatally blights its promise, my father most anxiously guarded against. This was self-conceit. He kept me, with extreme vigilance, out of the way of hearing myself praised, or of being led to make self-flattering comparisons between myself and others. From his own intercourse with me I could derive none but a very humble opinion of myself; and the standard of comparison he always held up to me was not what other people did, but what a man could and ought to do. He completely succeeded in preserving me from the sort of influences he so much dreaded. I was not at all aware that my attainments were anything unusual at my age. If I accidentally had my attention drawn to the fact that some other boy knew less than myself—which happened less often than might be imagined—I concluded not that I knew much, but that he, for some reason or other, knew little, or that his knowledge was of a different kind from mine. My state of mind was not humility, but neither was it arrogance. I never thought of saying to myself, I am, or I can do, so and so. I neither estimated myself highly nor lowly; I did not estimate myself at all. If I thought anything about myself, it was that I was rather backward in my studies, since I always found myself so, in comparison with what my father expected from me. I assert this with confidence, though it was not the impression of various persons who saw me in my childhood. They, as I have since found, thought me greatly and disagreeably self-conceited; probably because I was disputatious, and did not scruple to give direct contradictions to things which I heard said. I suppose I acquired this bad habit from having been encouraged in an unusual degree to talk on matters beyond my age, and with grown persons, while I never had inculcated on me the usual respect for them. My father did not correct this ill breeding and impertinence, probably from not being aware of it, for I was always too much in awe of him to be otherwise than extremely subdued and quiet in his presence. Yet with all this I had no notion of any superiority in myself; and well was it for me that I had not. I remember the very place in Hyde Park where, in my fourteenth year, on the eve of leaving my father's house for a long absence, he told me that I should find, as I got acquainted with new people, that I had been taught many things which youths of my age did not commonly know; and that many persons would be disposed to talk to me of this, and to compliment me upon it. What other things he said on this topic I remember very imperfectly; but he wound up by saying that whatever I knew more than others could not be ascribed to any merit in me, but to the very unusual advantage which had fallen to my lot of having a father who was able to teach me, and willing to give the necessary trouble and time; that it was no matter of praise to me if I knew more than those who had not had a similar advantage, but the deepest disgrace to me if I did not. I have a distinct remembrance that the suggestion thus for the first time made to me, that I knew more than other youths who were considered well educated, was to me a piece of information, to which, as to all other things which my father told me, I gave implicit credence, but which did not at all impress me as a personal matter. I felt no disposition to glorify myself upon the circumstance that there were other persons who did not know what I knew; nor had I ever flattered myself that my acquirements, whatever they might be, were any merit of mine; but, now when my attention was called to the subject, I felt that what my father had said respecting my peculiar advantages was exactly the truth and common sense of the matter, and it fixed my opinion and feeling from that time forward.

It is evident that this, among many other of the purposes of my father's scheme of education, could not have been accomplished if he had not carefully kept me from having any great amount of intercourse with other boys. He was earnestly bent upon my escaping not only the corrupting influence which boys exercise over boys, but the contagion of vulgar modes of thought and feeling; and for this he was willing that I should pay the price of inferiority in the accomplishments which schoolboys in all countries chiefly

cultivate. The deficiencies in my education were principally in the things which boys learn from being turned
out to shift for themselves, and from being brought together in large numbers. From temperance and much
walking, I grew up healthy and hardy, though not mus-
cular; but I could do no feats of skill or physical strength,
and knew none of the ordinary bodily exercises. It was not
that play, or time for it, was refused me. Though no
holidays were allowed, lest the habit of work should be
broken, and a taste for idleness acquired, I had ample
leisure in every day to amuse myself; but as I had no boy
companions, and the animal need of physical activity was
satisfied by walking, my amusements, which were mostly
solitary, were in general of a quiet, if not a bookish turn,
and gave little stimulus to any other kind even of mental
activity than that which was already called forth by my
studies; I consequently remained long, and in a less degree
have always remained, inexpert in anything requiring
manual dexterity; my mind, as well as my hands, did its
work very lamely when it was applied, or ought to have
been applied, to the practical details which, as they are
the chief interest of life to the majority of men, are also
the things in which whatever mental capacity they have
chiefly shows itself; I was constantly meriting reproof by
inattention, inobservance, and general slackness of mind
in matters of daily life. My father was the extreme opposite
in these particulars: his senses and mental faculties were
always on the alert; he carried decision and energy of
character in his whole manner and into every action of
life; and this, as much as his talents, contributed to the
strong impression which he always made upon those with
whom he came into personal contact. But the children
of energetic parents frequently grow up unenergetic, because they lean on their parents, and the parents are
energetic for them. The education which my father gave
me was in itself much more fitted for training me to *know*
than to *do*. Not that he was unaware of my deficiencies;
both as a boy and as a youth I was incessantly smarting
under his severe admonitions on the subject. There was
anything but insensibility or tolerance on his part towards
such shortcomings; but, while he saved me from the demoralizing effects of school life, he made no effort to provide me with any sufficient substitute for its practicalizing

influences. Whatever qualities he himself, probably, had acquired without difficulty or special training, he seems to have supposed that I ought to acquire as easily. He had not, I think, bestowed the same amount of thought and attention on this as on most other branches of education; and here, as well as in some other points of my tuition, he seems to have expected effects without causes.

MORAL INFLUENCES IN EARLY
YOUTH; MY FATHER'S CHARACTER
AND OPINIONS

In my education, as in that of every-
one, the moral influences, which are so much more important than all others, are also the most complicated, and
the most difficult to specify with any approach to completeness. Without attempting the hopeless task of detailing
the circumstances by which, in this respect, my early character may have been shaped, I shall confine myself to a
few leading points, which form an indispensable part of
any true account of my education.

I was brought up from the first without any religious
belief, in the ordinary acceptation of the term. My
father, educated in the creed of Scotch Presbyterianism,
had by his own studies and reflections been early led to
reject not only the belief in Revelation, but the foundations

of what is commonly called natural religion. I have heard him say, that the turning point of his mind on the subject was reading Butler's *Analogy*. That work, of which he always continued to speak with respect, kept him, as he said, for some considerable time, a believer in the divine authority of Christianity; by proving to him that whatever are the difficulties in believing that the Old and New Testaments proceed from, or record the acts of, a perfectly wise and good being, the same and still greater difficulties stand in the way of the belief that a being of such a character can have been the Maker of the universe. He considered Butler's argument as conclusive against the only opponents for whom it was intended. Those who admit an omnipotent as well as perfectly just and benevolent maker and ruler of such a world as this can say little against Christianity but what can, with at least equal force, be retorted against themselves. Finding, therefore, no halting place in deism, he remained in a state of perplexity, until, doubtless after many struggles, he yielded to the conviction that concerning the origin of things nothing whatever can be known. This is the only correct statement of his opinion; for dogmatic atheism he looked upon as absurd; as most of those whom the world has considered atheists have always done. These particulars are important, because they show that my father's rejection of all that is called religious belief was not, as many might suppose, primarily a matter of logic and evidence; the grounds of it were moral, still more than intellectual. He found it impossible to believe that a world so full of evil was the work of an Author combining infinite power with perfect goodness and righteousness. His intellect spurned the subtleties by which men attempt to blind themselves to this open contradiction. The Sabean, or Manichean theory of a Good and an Evil Principle, struggling against each other for the government of the universe, he would not have equally condemned; and I have heard him express surprise that no one revived it in our time. He would have regarded it as a mere hypothesis; but he would have ascribed to it no depraving influence. As it was, his aversion to religion, in the sense usually attached to the term, was of the same kind with that of Lucretius: he regarded it with the feelings due not to a mere mental delusion, but to a great moral evil. He looked upon it as

the greatest enemy of morality: first, by setting up fictitious
excellences—belief in creeds, devotional feelings, and
ceremonies, not connected with the good of humankind—
and causing these to be accepted as substitutes for genuine virtues; but above all, by radically vitiating the standard of morals; making it consist in doing the will of a
being, on whom it lavishes indeed all the phrases of
adulation, but whom in sober truth it depicts as eminently
hateful. I have a hundred times heard him say that all
ages and nations have represented their gods as wicked,
in a constantly increasing progression, that mankind have
gone on adding trait after trait till they reached the
most perfect conception of wickedness which the human
mind can devise, and have called this God, and prostrated
themselves before it. This *ne plus ultra* of wickedness he
considered to be embodied in what is commonly presented
to mankind as the creed of Christianity. Think (he used
to say) of a being who would make a hell—who would
create the human race with the infallible foreknowledge,
and therefore with the intention, that the great majority
of them were to be consigned to horrible and everlasting
torment. The time, I believe, is drawing near when this
dreadful conception of an object of worship will be no
longer identified with Christianity; and when all persons
with any sense of moral good and evil will look upon it
with the same indignation with which my father regarded
it. My father was as well aware as any one that Christians
do not, in general, undergo the demoralizing consequences
which seem inherent in such a creed, in the manner or to
the extent which might have been expected from it. The
same slovenliness of thought, and subjection of the reason
to fears, wishes, and affections, which enable them to
accept a theory involving a contradiction in terms, pre-
vents them from perceiving the logical consequences of
the theory. Such is the facility with which mankind believe at one and the same things inconsistent with one another, and so few are those who draw, from what they
receive as truths, any consequences but those recommended to them by their feelings that multitudes have
held the undoubting belief in an Omnipotent Author of
hell, and have nevertheless identified that being with the
best conception they were able to form of perfect goodness. Their worship was not paid to the demon which

such a Being as they imagined would really be, but to their own ideal of excellence. The evil is that such a belief keeps the ideal wretchedly low; and opposes the most obstinate resistance to all thought which has a tendency to raise it higher. Believers shrink from every train of ideas which would lead the mind to a clear conception and an elevated standard of excellence, because they feel (even when they do not distinctly see) that such a standard would conflict with many of the dispensations of nature, and with much of what they are accustomed to consider as the Christian creed. And thus morality continues a matter of blind tradition, with no consistent principle, nor even any consistent feeling, to guide it.

It would have been wholly inconsistent with my father's ideas of duty to allow me to acquire impressions contrary to his convictions and feelings respecting religion: and he impressed upon me from the first, that the manner in which the world came into existence was a subject on which nothing was known; that the question, "Who made me?" cannot be answered, because we have no experience or authentic information from which to answer it; and that any answer only throws the difficulty a step further back, since the question immediately presents itself, "Who made God?" He, at the same time, took care that I should be acquainted with what had been thought by mankind on these impenetrable problems. I have mentioned at how early an age he made me a reader of ecclesiastical history; and he taught me to take the strongest interest in the Reformation as the great and decisive contest against priestly tyranny for liberty of thought.

I am thus one of the very few examples, in this country, of one who has not thrown off religious belief, but never had it: I grew up in a negative state with regard to it. I looked upon the modern exactly as I did upon the ancient religion, as something which in no way concerned me. It did not seem to me more strange that English people should believe what I did not than that the men I read of in Herodotus should have done so. History had made the variety of opinions among mankind a fact familiar to me, and this was but a prolongation of that fact. This point in my early education had, however, incidentally one bad consequence deserving notice. In giving me an opinion contrary to that of the world, my father thought it necessary to give it as one which could not prudently be avowed to the world. This lesson of keeping my thoughts to myself, at that early age, was attended with some moral disadvantages; though my limited intercourse with strangers, especially such as were likely to speak to me on religion, prevented me from being placed in the alternative of avowal or hypocrisy. I remember two occasions in my boyhood on which I felt myself in this alternative, and in both cases I avowed my disbelief and defended it. My opponents were boys, considerably older than myself: one of them I certainly staggered at the time, but the subject was never renewed between us; the other, who was surprised and somewhat shocked, did his best to convince me for some time, without effect.

The great advance in liberty of discussion, which is one of the most important differences between the present time and that of my childhood, has greatly altered the moralities of this question; and I think that few men of my father's intellect and public spirit, holding, with such intensity of moral conviction as he did, unpopular opinions on religion, or on any other of the great subjects of thought, would now either practise or inculcate the withholding of them from the world, unless in the cases, becoming fewer every day, in which frankness on these subjects would either risk the loss of means of subsistence, or would amount to exclusion from some sphere of usefulness peculiarly suitable to the capacities of the individual. On religion in particular the time appears to me to have come when it is the duty of all who, being qualified in point of knowledge, have on mature consideration satisfied themselves that the current opinions are not only false but hurtful, to make their dissent known; at least, if they are among those whose station or reputation gives their opinion a chance of being attended to. Such an avowal would put an end, at once and forever, to the vulgar prejudice that what is called, very improperly, unbelief is connected with any bad qualities either of mind or heart. The world would be astonished if it knew how great a proportion of its brightest ornaments—of those most distinguished even in popular estimation for wisdom and virtue—are complete sceptics in religion; many of them refraining from avowal, less from personal considerations, than from a conscientious, though now in my opinion a most mistaken apprehension, lest by speaking out what would tend to weaken existing beliefs, and by consequence (as they suppose) existing restraints, they should do harm instead of good.

Of unbelievers (so called), as well as of believers, there are many species, including almost every variety of moral type. But the best among them, as no one who has had opportunities of really knowing them will hesitate to affirm, are more genuinely religious, in the best sense of the word religion, than those who exclusively arrogate to themselves the title. The liberality of the age, or in other words the weakening of the obstinate prejudice which makes men unable to see what is before their eyes because it is contrary to their expectations, has caused it to be very commonly admitted that a deist may be truly religious; but if religion stands for any graces of character and not for mere dogma, the assertion may equally be made of many whose belief is far short of deism. Though they may think the proof incomplete that the universe is a work of design, and though they assuredly disbelieve that it can have an Author and Governor who is *absolute* in power as well as perfect in goodness, they have that which constitutes the principal worth of all religions whatever, an ideal conception of a Perfect Being, to which they habitually refer as the guide of their conscience; and this ideal of Good is usually far nearer to perfection than the objective Deity of those who think themselves obliged to find absolute goodness in the Author of a world so crowded with suffering and so deformed by injustice as ours.

My father's moral convictions, wholly dissevered from religion, were very much of the character of those of the Greek philosophers; and were delivered with the force and decision which characterized all that came from him. Even at the very early age at which I read with him the *Memorabilia* of Xenophon, I imbibed from that work and from his comments a deep respect for the character of Socrates, who stood in my mind as a model of ideal excellence; and I well remember how my father at that time impressed upon me the lesson of the choice of Hercules. At a somewhat later period the lofty moral standard exhibited in the writings of Plato operated upon me with great force. My father's moral inculcations were at all times mainly those of the *Socratici viri*: justice, temperance (to which he gave a very extended application), veracity, perseverance, readiness to encounter pain and especially labour; regard for the public good; estimation of persons according to their merits, and of things according to their intrinsic usefulness; a life of exertion in contradiction to one of self-indulgent ease and sloth. These and other moralities he conveyed in brief sentences, uttered as occasion arose, of grave exhortation, or stern reprobation and contempt.

But though direct moral teaching does much, indirect does more; and the effect my father produced on my character did not depend solely on what he said or did with that direct object, but also, and still more, on what manner of man he was.

In his views of life he partook of the character of the Stoic, the Epicurean, and the Cynic, not in the modern but the ancient sense of the word. In his personal qualities the Stoic predominated. His standard of morals was Epicurean, inasmuch as it was utilitarian, taking as the exclusive test of right and wrong the tendency of actions to produce pleasure or pain. But he had (and this was the Cynic element) scarcely any belief in pleasure; at least in his later years, of which alone, on this point, I can speak confidently. He was not insensible to pleasures; but he deemed very few of them worth the price which, at least in the present state of society, must be paid for them. The greater number of miscarriages in life he considered to be attributable to the overvaluing of pleasures. Accordingly, temperance, in the large sense intended by the Greek philosophers—stopping short at the point of moderation in all indulgences—was with him, as with them, almost the central point of educational precept. His inculcations of this virtue fill a large place in my childish remembrances. He thought human life a poor thing at best, after the freshness of youth and of unsatisfied curiosity had gone by. This was a topic on which he did not often speak, especially, it may be supposed, in the presence of young persons; but when he did, it was with an air of settled and profound conviction. He would sometimes say that if life were made what it might be, by good government and good education, it would be worth having; but he never spoke with anything like enthusiasm even of that possibility. He never varied in rating intellectual enjoyments above all others, even in value as pleasures, independently of their ulterior benefits. The pleasures of the benevolent affections he placed high in the scale; and used to say that he had never known a happy old man, except those who were able to live over again in the pleasures of the young. For passionate emotions of all sorts, and for everything which has been said or written in exaltation of them, he professed the greatest contempt. He regarded them as a form of madness. The "intense" was with him a by-word of scornful disapprobation. He regarded as an aberration of the moral standard of modern times, compared with that of the ancients, the great stress laid upon feeling. Feelings, as such, he considered to be no proper subjects of praise or blame. Right and wrong, good and bad, he regarded as qualities solely of conduct— of acts and omissions; there being no feeling which may not lead, and does not frequently lead, either to good, or to bad actions; conscience itself, the very desire to act right, often leading people to act wrong. Consistently carrying out the doctrine that the object of praise and blame should be the discouragement of wrong conduct and the encouragement of right, he refused to let his praise or blame be influenced by the motive of the agent. He blamed as severely what he thought a bad action, when the motive was a feeling of duty, as if the agents had been consciously evil doers. He would not have accepted as a plea in mitigation for inquisitors that they sincerely believed burning heretics to be an obligation of conscience. But though he did not allow honesty of purpose to soften his disapprobation of actions, it had its full effect on his estimation of characters. No one prized conscientiousness and rectitude of intention more highly, or was more incapable of valuing any person in whom he did not feel assurance of it. But he disliked people quite as much for any other deficiency, provided he thought it equally likely to make them act ill. He disliked, for instance, a fanatic in any bad cause, as much or more than one who adopted the same cause from self-interest, because he thought him even more likely to be practically mischievous. And thus, his aversion to many intellectual errors, or what he regarded as such, partook, in a certain sense, of the character of a moral feeling. All this is merely saying that he, in a degree once common, but now very unusual, threw his feelings into his opinions; which truly it is difficult to understand how any one who possesses much of both can fail to do. None but those who do not care about opinions will confound this with intolerance. Those who, having opinions which they hold to be immensely important, and their contraries to be prodigiously hurtful, have any deep regard for the general good, will necessarily dislike, as a class and in the abstract, those who think wrong what they think right, and right what they think wrong; though they need not therefore be, nor was my father, insensible to good qualities in an opponent, nor governed in their estimation of individuals by one general presumption, instead of by the whole of their character. I grant that an earnest person, being no more infallible than other men, is liable to dislike people on account of opinions which do not merit dislike; but if he neither himself does them any ill office, nor connives at its being done by others, he is not intolerant; and the forbearance which flows from a conscientious sense of the importance to mankind of the equal freedom of all opinions is the only tolerance which is commendable, or, to the highest moral order of minds, possible.

It will be admitted that a man of the opinions, and the character, above described, was likely to leave a strong moral impression on any mind principally formed by him, and that his moral teaching was not likely to err on the side of laxity or indulgence. The element which was chiefly deficient in his moral relation to his children was that of tenderness. I do not believe that this deficiency lay in his own nature. I believe him to have had much more feeling than he habitually showed, and much greater capacities of feeling than were ever developed. He resembled most Englishmen in being ashamed of the signs of feeling, and, by the absence of demonstration, starving the feelings themselves. If we consider further that he was in the trying position of sole teacher, and add to this that his temper was constitutionally irritable, it is impossible not to feel true pity for a father who did, and strove to do, so much for his children, who would have so valued their affection, yet who must have been constantly feeling that fear of him was drying it up at its source. This was no longer the case later in life, and with his younger children. They loved him tenderly; and if I cannot say so much of myself, I was always loyally devoted to him. As regards my own education, I hesitate to pronounce whether I was more a loser or gainer by his severity. It was not such as to prevent me from having a happy childhood. And I do not believe that boys can be induced to apply themselves with vigour, and what is so much more difficult, perseverance, to dry and irksome studies, by the sole force of persuasion and soft words. Much must be done, and much must be learnt, by children, for which rigid discipline and known liability to punishment, are indispensable as means. It is, no doubt, a very laudable effort, in modern teaching, to render as much as possible of what the young are required to learn, easy and interesting to them. But when this principle is pushed to the length of not requiring them to learn anything *but* what has been made easy and interesting, one of the chief objects of education is sacrificed. I rejoice in the decline of the old brutal and tyrannical system of teaching, which, however, did succeed in enforcing habits of application; but the new, as it seems to me, is training up a race of men who will be incapable of doing anything which is disagreeable to them. I do not, then, believe that fear, as an element in education, can be dispensed with; but I am sure that it ought not to be the main element; and when it predominates so much as to preclude love and confidence on the part of the child to those who should be the unreservedly trusted advisers of after years, and perhaps to seal up the fountains of frank and spontaneous communicativeness in the child's nature, it is an evil for which a large abatement must be made from the benefits, moral and intellectual, which may flow from any other part of the education.

During this first period of my life, the habitual frequenters of my father's house were limited to a very few persons, most of them little known to the world, but whom personal worth, and more or less of congeniality with at least his political opinions (not so frequently to be met with then as since) inclined him to cultivate; and his conversations with them I listened to with interest and instruction. My being an habitual inmate of my father's study made me acquainted with the dearest of his friends, David Ricardo, who by his benevolent countenance, and kindliness of manner, was very attractive to young per-

...s, and who, after I became a student of political economy, invited me to his house and to walk with him in order
to converse on the subject. I was a more frequent visitor
(from about 1817 or 1818) to Mr. Hume, who, born in
the same part of Scotland as my father, and having been,
I rather think, a younger schoolfellow or college companion of his, had on returning from India renewed their
youthful acquaintance, and who, coming like many others
greatly under the influence of my father's intellect and
energy of character, was induced partly by that influence
to go into Parliament, and there adopt the line of conduct which has given him an honourable place in the
history of this country. Of Mr. Bentham I saw much more,
owing to the close intimacy which existed between him
and my father. I do not know how soon after my father's
first arrival in England they became acquainted. But my
father was the earliest Englishman of any great mark who
thoroughly understood, and in the main adopted, Bentham's general views of ethics, government, and law; and
this was a natural foundation for sympathy between them,
and made them familiar companions in a period of Bentham's life during which he admitted much fewer visitors
than was the case subsequently. At this time Mr. Bentham
passed some part of every year at Barrow Green House,
in a beautiful part of the Surrey Hills, a few miles from
Godstone, and there I each summer accompanied my
father in a long visit. In 1813 Mr. Bentham, my father,
and I made an excursion, which included Oxford, Bath
and Bristol, Exeter, Plymouth, and Portsmouth. In this
journey I saw many things which were instructive to
me, and acquired my first taste for natural scenery,
in the elementary form of fondness for a "view." In the
succeeding winter we moved into a house very near Mr.
Bentham's, which my father rented from him, in Queen
Square, Westminster. From 1814 to 1817 Mr. Bentham
lived during half of each year at Ford Abbey, in Somersetshire (or rather in a part of Devonshire surrounded
by Somersetshire), which intervals I had the advantage
of passing at that place. This sojourn was, I think, an important circumstance in my education. Nothing contributes more to nourish elevation of sentiments in a people
than the large and free character of their habitations.
The middle-age architecture, the baronial hall, and the

spacious and lofty rooms of this fine old place, so unlike the mean and cramped externals of English middle
class life, gave the sentiment of a larger and freer existence,
and were to me a sort of poetic cultivation, aided also by
the character of the grounds in which the Abbey stood;
which were riant and secluded, umbrageous, and full of
the sound of falling waters.

I owed another of the fortunate circumstances in my
education, a year's residence in France, to Mr. Bentham's brother, General Sir Samuel Bentham. I had seen
Sir Samuel Bentham and his family at their house near
Gosport in the course of the tour already mentioned (he
being then Superintendent of the Dockyard at Portsmouth), and during a stay of a few days which they
made at Ford Abbey shortly after the peace, before going
to live on the Continent. In 1820 they invited me for a
six months' visit to them in the South of France, which
their kindness ultimately prolonged to nearly a twelve-
month. Sir Samuel Bentham, though of a character of
mind different from that of his illustrious brother, was
a man of very considerable attainments and general
powers, with a decided genius for mechanical art.
His wife, a daughter of the celebrated chemist, Dr.
Fordyce, was a woman of strong will and decided character, much general knowledge, and great practical good
sense of the Edgeworth kind: she was the ruling spirit of
the household, as she deserved, and was well qualified, to
be. Their family consisted of one son (the eminent botan-
ist) and three daughters, the youngest about two years my
senior. I am indebted to them for much and various instruction, and for an almost parental interest in my wel-
fare. When I first joined them, in May 1820, they
occupied the Château of Pompignan (still belonging to a
descendant of Voltaire's enemy), on the heights overlook-
ing the plain of the Garonne between Montauban and
Toulouse. I accompanied them in an excursion to the
Pyrenees, including a stay of some duration at Bagnères
de Bigorre, a journey to Pau, Bayonne, and Bagnères de
Luchon, and an ascent of the Pic du Midi de Bigorre.

This first introduction to the highest order of mountain
scenery made the deepest impression on me, and gave a
colour to my tastes through life. In October we proceeded
by the beautiful mountain route of Castres and St. Pons,

...n Toulouse to Montpellier, in which last neighbourhood Sir Samuel had just bought the estate of Restinclière,
near the foot of the singular mountain of St. Loup. During
this residence in France I acquired a familiar knowledge
of the French language, and acquaintance with the ordinary
French literature; I took lessons in various bodily exercises, in none of which however I made any proficiency; and at Montepellier I attended the excellent winter
courses of lectures at the Faculté des Sciences, those of
M. Anglada on chemistry, of M. Provençal on zoology,
and of a very accomplished representative of the eighteenth
century metaphysics, M. Gergonne, on logic, under the
name of Philosophy of the Sciences. I also went through a
course of the higher mathematics under the private tuition
of M. Lenthéric, a professor at the Lycée of Montpellier.
But the greatest, perhaps, of the many advantages which
I owed to this episode in my education was that of having breathed, for a whole year, the free and genial
atmosphere of continental life. This advantage was not
the less real though I could not then estimate, nor even
consciously feel it. Having so little experience of English
life, and the few people I knew being mostly such as had
public objects, of a large and personally disinterested
kind, at heart, I was ignorant of the low moral tone of
what, in England, is called society: the habit of, not indeed professing, but taking for granted in every mode of
implication that conduct is of course always directed towards low and petty objects; the absence of high feelings
which manifests itself by sneering depreciation of all
demonstrations of them, and by general abstinence (except among a few of the stricter religionists) from professing any high principles of action at all, except in those
pre-ordained cases in which such profession is put on as
part of the costume and formalities of the occasion. I could
not then know or estimate the difference between this
manner of existence and that of a people like the French,
whose faults, if equally real, are at all events different;
among whom sentiments, which by comparison at least
may be called elevated, are the current coin of human
intercourse, both in books and in private life; and, though
often evaporating in profession, are yet kept alive in the
nation at large by constant exercise, and stimulated by
sympathy, so as to form a living and active part of the

existence of great numbers of persons, and to be recognized and understood by all. Neither could I then appreciate the general culture of the understanding, which results from the habitual exercise of the feelings, and is thus carried down into the most uneducated classes of several countries on the Continent, in a degree not equalled in England among the so-called educated, except where an unusual tenderness of conscience leads to an habitual exercise of the intellect on questions of right and wrong. I did not know the way in which, among the ordinary English, the absence of interest in things of an unselfish kind, except occasionally in a special thing here and there, and the habit of not speaking to others, nor much even to themselves, about the things in which they do feel interest, causes both their feelings and their intellectual faculties to remain undeveloped, or to develop themselves only in some single and very limited direction; reducing them, considered as spiritual beings, to a kind of negative existence. All these things I did not perceive till long afterwards; but I even then felt, though without stating it clearly to myself, the contrast between the frank sociability and amiability of French personal intercourse and the English mode of existence in which everybody acts as if everybody else (with few, or no exceptions) was either an enemy or a bore. In France, it is true, the bad as well as the good points, both of individual and of national character, come more to the surface, and break out more fearlessly in ordinary intercourse than in England; but the general habit of the people is to show, as well as to expect, friendly feeling in every one towards every other, wherever there is not some positive cause for the opposite. In England it is only of the best bred people, in the upper or upper middle ranks, that anything like this can be said.

In my way through Paris, both going and returning, I passed some time in the house of M. Say, the eminent political economist, who was a friend and correspondent of my father, having become acquainted with him on a visit to England a year or two after the peace. He was a man of the later period of the French Revolution, a fine specimen of the best kind of French Republican, one of those who had never bent the knee to Bonaparte though courted by him to do so; a truly upright, brave, and enlightened man. He lived a quiet and studious life, made happy by warm affections, public and private. He was acquainted with many of the chiefs of the Liberal party, and I saw various noteworthy persons while staying at his house; among whom I have pleasure in the recollection of having once seen Saint-Simon, not yet the founder either of a philosophy or a religion, and considered only as a clever original. The chief fruit which I carried away from the society I saw, was a strong and permanent interest in continental liberalism, of which I ever afterwards kept myself *au courant,* as much as of English politics: a thing not at all usual in those days with Englishmen, and which had a very salutary influence on my development, keeping me free from the error always prevalent in England, and from which even my father with all his superiority to prejudice was not exempt, of judging universal questions by a merely English standard. After passing a few weeks at Caen with an old friend of my father's, I returned to England in July 1821; and my education resumed its ordinary course.

CHAPTER III   1821-1823

LAST STAGE OF EDUCATION, AND
FIRST OF SELF-EDUCATION

For the first year or two after my visit to
France, I continued my old studies, with the addition of
some new ones. When I returned, my father was just
finishing for the press his *Elements of Political Economy,*
and he made me perform an exercise on the manuscript,
which Mr. Bentham practised on all his own writings,
making what he called "marginal contents": a short abstract of every paragraph, to enable the writer more easily
to judge of, and improve, the order of the ideas, and the
general character of the exposition. Soon after, my father
put into my hands Condillac's *Traité des Sensations,*
and the logical and metaphysical volumes of his *Cours
d'Etudes;* the first (notwithstanding the superficial resemblance between Condillac's psychological system and
my father's), quite as much for a warning as for an example. I am not sure whether it was in this winter or the

63

next that I first read a history of the French Revolution.
I learnt, with astonishment, that the principles of democracy, then apparently in so insignificant and hopeless a
minority everywhere in Europe, had borne all before them
in France thirty years earlier, and had been the creed of
the nation. As may be supposed from this, I had previously a very vague idea of that great commotion. I knew
only that the French had thrown off the absolute monarchy
of Louis XIV and XV, had put the King and Queen to
death, guillotined many persons, one of whom was La-
voisier, and had ultimately fallen under the despotism of
Bonaparte. From this time, as was natural, the subject
took an immense hold of my feelings. It allied itself with
all my juvenile aspirations to the character of a democratic
champion. What had happened so lately seemed as if it
might easily happen again; and the most transcendent
glory I was capable of conceiving was that of figuring,
successful or unsuccessful, as a Girondist in an English
convention.

During the winter of 1821-22, Mr. John Austin, with
whom at the time of my visit to France my father had
but lately become acquainted, kindly allowed me to read
Roman law with him. My father, notwithstanding his
abhorrence of the chaos of barbarism called English law,
had turned his thoughts towards the bar as on the whole
less ineligible for me than any other profession; and these
readings with Mr. Austin, who had made Bentham's best
ideas his own, and added much to them from other sources
and from his own mind, were not only a valuable introduction to legal studies, but an important portion of
general education. With Mr. Austin I read Heineccius
on the *Institutes,* his *Roman Antiquities,* and part of his
exposition of the *Pandects*; to which was added a considerable portion of Blackstone. It was at the commencement
of these studies that my father, as a needful accompani-
ment to them, put into my hands Bentham's principal
speculations, as interpreted to the Continent, and indeed
to all the world, by Dumont, in the *Traité de Législation.*
The reading of this book was an epoch in my life; one of
the turning points in my mental history.

My previous education had been, in a certain sense,
already a course of Benthamism. The Benthamic standard
of "the greatest happiness" was that which I had always-

been taught to apply; I was even familiar with an abstract discussion of it, forming an episode in an unpublished dialogue on government, written by my father on the Platonic model. Yet in the first pages of Bentham it burst upon me with all the force of novelty. What thus impressed me was the chapter in which Bentham passed judgment on the common modes of reasoning in morals and legislation, deduced from phrases like "law of nature," "right reason," "the moral sense," "natural rectitude," and the like, and characterized them as dogmatism in disguise, imposing its sentiments upon others under cover of sounding expressions which convey no reason for the sentiment, but set up the sentiment as its own reason. It had not struck me before that Bentham's principle put an end to all this. The feeling rushed upon me that all previous moralists were superseded, and that here indeed was the commencement of a new era in thought. This impression was strengthened by the manner in which Bentham put into scientific form the application of the happiness principle to the morality of actions, by analysing the various classes and orders of their consequences. But what struck me at that time most of all was the "Classification of Offences," which is much more clear, compact and imposing in Dumont's redaction than in the original work of Bentham from which it was taken. Logic and the dialectics of Plato, which had formed so large a part of my previous training, had given me a strong relish for accurate classification. This taste had been strengthened and enlightened by the study of botany, on the principles of what is called the natural method, which I had taken up with great zeal, though only as an amusement, during my stay in France; and when I found scientific classification applied to the great and complex subject of punishable acts, under the guidance of the ethical principle of pleasurable and painful consequences, followed out in the method of detail introduced into these subjects by Bentham, I felt taken up to an eminence from which I could survey a vast mental domain, and see stretching out into the distance intellectual results beyond all computation. As I proceeded further, there seemed to be added to this intellectual clearness the most inspiring prospects of practical improvement in human affairs. To Bentham's general view of the construction of a body of law I was not altogether a stranger, having read with attention that admirable compendium, my father's article on jurisprudence; but I had read it with little profit, and scarcely any interest, no doubt from its extremely general and abstract character, and also because it concerned the form more than the substance of the corpus juris, the logic rather than the ethics of law. But Bentham's subject was legislation, of which jurisprudence is only the formal part; and at every page he seemed to open a clearer and broader conception of what human opinions and institutions ought to be, how they might be made what they ought to be, and how far removed from it they now are. When I laid down the last volume of the *Traité,* I had become a different being. The "principle of utility" understood as Bentham understood it, and applied in the manner in which he applied it through these three volumes, fell exactly into its place as the keystone which held together the detached and fragmentary component parts of my knowledge and beliefs. It gave unity to my conceptions of things. I now had opinions; a creed, a doctrine, a philosophy; in one among the best senses of the word, a religion; the inculcation and diffusion of which could be made the principal outward purpose of a life. And I had a grand conception laid before me of changes to be effected in the condition of mankind through that doctrine. The *Traité de Législation* wound up with what was to me a most impressive picture of human life as it would be made by such opinions and such laws as were recommended in the treatise. The anticipations of practicable improvement were studiously moderate, deprecating and discountenancing as reveries of vague enthusiasm many things which will one day seem so natural to human beings that injustice will probably be done to those who once thought them chimerical. But, in my state of mind, this appearance of superiority to illusion added to the effect which Bentham's doctrines produced on me, by heightening the impression of mental power, and the vista of improvement which he did open, was sufficiently large and brilliant to light up my life, as well as to give a definite shape to my aspirations.

After this I read, from time to time, the most important of the other works of Bentham which had then seen the light, either as written by himself or as edited by Dumont. This was my private reading; while, under my father's direction, my studies were carried into the higher branches of analytic psychology. I now read Lock's *Essay,* and wrote out an account of it, consisting of a complete abstract of every chapter, with such remarks as occurred to me; which was read by, or (I think) to, my father, and discussed throughout. I performed the same process with Helvétius' *de l'Esprit,* which I read of my own choice. This preparation of abstracts, subject to my father's censorship, was of great service to me, by compelling precision in conceiving and expressing psychological doctrines, whether accepted as truths or only regarded as the opinion of others. After Helvétius, my father made me study what he deemed the really master-production in the philosophy of mind, Hartley's *Observations on Man.* This book, though it did not, like the *Traité de Législation,* give a new colour to my existence, made a very similar impression on me in regard to its immediate subject. Hartley's explanation, incomplete as in many points it is, of the more complex mental phenomena by the law of association, commended itself to me at once as a real analysis, and made me feel by contrast the insufficiency of the merely verbal generalizations of Condillac, and even of the instructive gropings and feelings about for psychological explanations, of Locke. It was at this very time that my father commenced writing his *Analysis of the Mind,* which carried Hartley's mode of explaining the mental phenomena to so much greater length and depth. He could only command the concentration of thought necessary for this work during the complete leisure of his holiday of a month or six weeks annually; and he commenced it in the summer of 1822, in the first holiday he passed at Dorking; in which neighbourhood, from that time to the end of his life, with the exception of two years, he lived, as far as his official duties permitted, for six months of every year. He worked at the *Analysis* during several successive vacations, up to the year 1829 when it was published, and allowed me to read the manuscript, portion by portion, as it advanced. The other principal English writers on mental philosophy I read as I felt inclined, particularly Berkeley, Hume's *Essays,* Reid, Dugald Stewart and Brown on *Cause and Effect.* Brown's *Lectures* I did not read until two or three years later, nor at that time had my father himself read them.

Among the works read in the course of this year, which contributed materially to my development, I ought to mention a book (written on the foundation of some of Bentham's manuscripts and published under the pseudonym of Philip Beauchamp) entitled *Analysis of the Influence of Natural Religion on the Temporal Happiness of Mankind.* This was an examination not of the truth, but of the usefulness of religious belief, in the most general sense, apart from the peculiarities of any special revelation; which, of all the parts of the discussion concerning religion, is the most important in this age, in which real belief in any religious doctrine is feeble and precarious, but the opinion of its necessity for moral and social purposes almost universal; and when those who reject revelation very generally take refuge in an optimistic deism, a worship of the order of Nature, and the supposed course of Providence, at least as full of contradictions, and perverting to the moral sentiments, as any of the forms of Christianity, if only it is as completely realized. Yet, very little, with any claim to a philosophical character, has been written by sceptics against the usefulness of this form of belief. The volume bearing the name of Philip Beauchamp had this for its special object. Having been shown to my father in manuscript, it was put into my hands by him, and I made a marginal analysis of it as I had done of the *Elements of Political Economy.* Next to the *Traité de Législation,* it was one of the books which by the searching character of its analysis produced the greatest effect upon me. On reading it lately after an interval of many years, I find it to have some of the defects as well as the merits of the Benthamic modes of thought, and to contain, as I now think, many weak arguments, but with a great overbalance of sound ones, and much good material for a more completely philosophic and conclusive treatment of the subject.

I have now, I believe, mentioned all the books which had any considerable effect on my early mental development. From this point I began to carry on my intellectual cultivation by writing still more than by reading. In the summer of 1822 I wrote my first argumentative essay. I remember very little about it, except that it was an attack on what I regarded as the aristocratic prejudice that the rich were, or were likely to be, superior in moral

qualities to the poor. My performance was entirely argumentative, without any of the declamation which the
subject would admit of, and might be expected to suggest
to a young writer. In that department, however, I was,
and remained, very inapt. Dry argument was the only
thing I could manage, or willingly attempted; though pas-
sively I was very susceptible to the effect of all composition,
whether in the form of poetry or oratory, which appealed
to the feelings on any basis of reason. My father, who
knew nothing of this essay until it was finished, was well
satisfied, and as I learnt from others, even pleased with
it; but, perhaps from a desire to promote the exercise of
other mental faculties than the purely logical, he advised
me to make my next exercise in composition one of the
oratorical kind: on which suggestion, availing myself of
my familiarity with Greek history and ideas and with
the Athenian orators, I wrote two speeches, one an accu-
sation, the other a defence of Pericles, on a supposed
impeachment for not marching out to fight the Lacedae-
monians on their invasion of Attica. After this I continued to write papers on subjects often very much
beyond my capacity, but with great benefit both from the
exercise itself, and from the discussions which it led to
with my father.

I had now also begun to converse, on general subjects,
with the instructed men with whom I came in contact;
and the opportunities of such contact naturally became
more numerous. The two friends of my father from
whom I derived most, and with whom I most associated,
were Mr. Grote and Mr. John Austin. The acquaintance
of both with my father was recent, but had ripened rapidly
into intimacy. Mr. Grote was introduced to my father by
Mr. Ricardo, I think in 1819 (being then about twenty-
five years old), and sought assiduously his society and
conversation. Already a highly instructed man, he was
yet, by the side of my father, a tyro in the great subjects
of human opinion; but he rapidly seized on my father's
best ideas; and in the department of political opinion he
made himself known as early as 1820 by a pamphlet in
defence of *Radical Reform,* in reply to a celebrated article
by Sir James Mackintosh, then lately published in the
Edinburgh Review. Mr. Grote's father, the banker, was,
I believe, a thorough Tory, and his mother intensely

Evangelical; so that for his liberal opinions he was in no way indebted to home influences. But, unlike most persons who have the prospect of being rich by inheritance, he had, though actively engaged in the business of banking, devoted a great portion of time to philosophic studies; and his intimacy with my father did much to decide the character of the next stage in his mental progress. Him I often visited, and my conversations with him on political, moral, and philosophical subjects gave me, in addition to much valuable instruction, all the pleasure and benefit of sympathetic communion with a man of the high intellectual and moral eminence which his life and writings have since manifested to the world.

Mr. Austin, who was four or five years older than Mr. Grote, was the eldest son of a retired miller in Suffolk, who had made money by contracts during the war, and who must have been a man or remarkable qualities, as I infer from the fact that all his sons were of more than common ability and all eminently gentlemen. The one with whom we are now concerned, and whose writings on jurisprudence have made him celebrated, was for some time in the army, and served in Sicily under Lord William Bentinck. After the peace he sold his commission and studied for the bar, to which he had been called for some time before my father knew him. He was not, like Mr. Grote, to any extent, a pupil of my father, but he had attained, by reading and thought, a considerable number of the same opinions, modified by his own very decided individuality of character. He was a man of great intellectual powers which in conversation appeared at their very best: from the vigour and richness of expression with which, under the excitement of discussion, he was accustomed to maintain some view or other of most general subjects; and from an appearance of not only strong, but deliberate and collected will; mixed with a certain bitterness, partly derived from temperament, and partly from the general cast of his feelings and reflections. The dissatisfaction with life and the world, felt more or less in the present state of society and intellect by every discerning and highly conscientious mind, gave in his case a rather melancholy tinge to the character, very natural to those whose passive moral susceptibilities are more than proportioned to their active energies. For it must be said that the strength of will, of which his manner seemed to give such strong assurance, expended itself principally in manner. With great zeal for human improvement, a strong sense of duty, and capacities and acquirements the extent of which is proved by the writings he has left, he hardly ever completed any intellectual task of magnitude. He had so high a standard of what ought to be done, so exaggerated a sense of deficiencies in his own performances, and was so unable to content himself with the amount of elaboration sufficient for the occasion and the purpose, that he not only spoilt much of his work for ordinary use by overlabouring it, but spent so much time and exertion in superfluous study and thought that when his task ought to have been completed, he had generally worked himself into an illness, without having half finished what he undertook. From this mental infirmity (of which he is not the sole example among the accomplished and able men whom I have known), combined with liability to frequent attacks of disabling though not dangerous ill health, he accomplished, through life, little in comparison with what he seemed capable of; but what he did produce is held in the very highest estimation by the most competent judges; and, like Coleridge, he might plead as a set-off that he had been to many persons, through his conversation, a source not only of much instruction but of great elevation of character. On me his influence was most salutary. It was moral in the best sense. He took a sincere and kind interest in me, far beyond what could have been expected towards a mere youth from a man of his age, standing, and what seemed austerity of character. There was in his conversation and demeanour a tone of high-mindedness which did not show itself so much, if the quality existed as much, in any of the other persons with whom at that time I associated. My intercourse with him was the more beneficial, owing to his being of a different mental type from all other intellectual men whom I frequented, and he from the first set himself decidedly against the prejudices and narrownesses which are almost sure to be found in a young man formed by a particular mode of thought or a particular social circle.

His younger brother, Charles Austin, of whom at this time and for the next year or two I saw much, had also a great effect on me, though of a very different description.

He was but a few years older than myself, and had then just left the University, where he had shone with great éclat as a man of intellect and a brilliant orator and converser. The effect he produced on his Cambridge contemporaries deserves to be accounted an historical event; for to it may in part be traced the tendency towards liberalism in general, and the Benthamic and politico-economic form of it in particular, which showed itself in a portion of the more active-minded young men of the higher classes from this time to 1830. The Union Debating Society, at that time at the height of its reputation, was an arena where what were then thought extreme opinions, in politics and philosophy, were weekly asserted, face to face with their opposites, before audiences consisting of the élite of the Cambridge youth; and though many persons afterwards of more or less note (of whom Lord Macaulay is the most celebrated), gained their first oratorical laurels in those debates, the really influential mind among these intellectual gladiators was Charles Austin. He continued, after leaving the University, to be, by his conversation and personal ascendancy, a leader among the same class of young men who had been his associates there; and he attached me among others to his car. Through him I became acquainted with Macaulay, Hyde and Charles Villiers, Strutt (now Lord Belper), Romilly (now Lord Romilly and Master of the Rolls), and various others who subsequently figured in literature or politics, and among whom I heard discussions on many topics, as yet to a certain degree new to me. The influence of Charles Austin over me differed from that of the persons I have hitherto mentioned, in being not the influence of a man over a boy, but that of an elder contemporary. It was through him that I first felt myself not a pupil under teachers, but a man among men. He was the first person of intellect whom I met on a ground of equality, though as yet much his inferior on that common ground. He was a man who never failed to impress greatly those with whom he came in contact, even when their opinions were the very reverse of his. The impression he gave was that of boundless strength, together with talents which, combined with such apparent force of will and character, seemed capable of dominating the world. Those who knew him, whether friendly to him or not, always anticipated that he would play a conspicu-

ous part in public life. It is seldom that men produce
so great an immediate effect by speech, unless they, in
some degree, lay themselves out for it; and he did this in
no ordinary degree. He loved to strike, and even to
startle. He knew that decision is the greatest element of
effect, and he uttered his opinions with all the decision he
could throw into them, never so well pleased as when he
astonished any one by their audacity. Very unlike his
brother, who made war against the narrower interpretations and applications of the principles they both professed, he, on the contrary, presented the Benthamic
doctrines in the most startling form of which they were susceptible, exaggerating everything in them which tended to
consequences offensive to any one's preconceived feelings.
All which he defended with such verve and vivacity, and
carried off by a manner so agreeable as well as forcible,
that he always either came off victor, or divided the
honours of the field. It is my belief that much of the
notion popularly entertained of the tenets and sentiments
of what are called Benthamites or Utilitarians had its
origin in paradoxes thrown out by Charles Austin. It
must be said, however, that his example was followed,
haud passibus aequis, by younger proselytes, and that to
outrer whatever was by anybody considered offensive in
the doctrines and maxims of Benthamism became at one
time the badge of a small coterie of youths. All of these
who had anything in them, myself among others, quickly
outgrew this boyish vanity; and those who had not, became tired of differing from other people, and gave up
both the good and the bad part of the heterodox opinions
they had for some time professed.

It was in the winter of 1822-23 that I formed the plan
of a little society, to be composed of young men agreeing
in fundamental principles—acknowledging utility as their
standard in ethics and politics, and a certain number of
the principal corollaries drawn from it in the philosophy
I had accepted—and meeting once a fortnight to read
essays and discuss questions conformably to the premises
thus agreed on. The fact would hardly be worth men-
tioning, but for the circumstance, that the name I gave
to the society I had planned was the Utilitarian Society. It
was the first time that any one had taken the title of
Utilitarian; and the term made its way into the language,

from this humble source. I did not invent the word, but found it in one of Galt's novels, the *Annals of the Parish*, in which the Scotch clergyman, of whom the book is a supposed autobiography, is represented as warning his parishioners not to leave the Gospel and become utilitarians. With a boy's fondness for a name and a banner I seized on the word, and for some years called myself and others by it as a sectarian appellation; and it came to be occasionally used by some others holding the opinions which it was intended to designate. As those opinions attracted more notice, the term was repeated by strangers and opponents, and got into rather common use just about the time when those who had originally assumed it laid down that along with other sectarian characteristics. The Society so called consisted at first of no more than three members, one of whom, being Mr. Bentham's amanuensis, obtained for us permission to hold our meetings in his house. The number never, I think, reached ten, and the society was broken up in 1826. It had thus an existence of about three years and a half. The chief effect of it as regards myself, over and above the benefit of practice in oral discussion, was that of bringing me in contact with several young men at that time less advanced than myself, among whom, as they professed the same opinions, I was for some time a sort of leader, and had considerable influence on their mental progress. Any young man of education who fell in my way, and whose opinions were not incompatible with those of the Society, I endeavoured to press into its service; and some others I probably should never have known, had they not joined it. Those of the members who became my intimate companions— no one of whom was in any sense of the word a disciple, but all of them independent thinkers on their own basis— were William Eyton Tooke, son of the eminent political economist, a young man of singular worth both moral and intellectual, lost to the world by an early death; his friend William Ellis, an original thinker in the field of political economy, now honourably known by his apostolic exertions for the improvement of education; George Graham, afterwards official assignee of the Bankruptcy Court, a thinker of originality and power on almost all abstract subjects; and (from the time when he came first to England to study for the bar in 1824 or 1825) a

man who has made considerably more noise in the world
than any of these, John Arthur Roebuck.

In May, 1823, my professional occupation and status
for the next thirty-five years of my life, were decided by
my father's obtaining for me an appointment from the
East India Company, in the office of the Examiner of
India Correspondence, immediately under himself. I was
appointed in the usual manner, at the bottom of the list
of clerks, to rise, at least in the first instance, by seniority;
but with the understanding that I should be employed
from the beginning in preparing drafts of dispatches, and
be thus trained up as a successor to those who then filled
the higher departments of the office. My drafts of course
required, for some time, much revision from my immediate superiors, but I soon became well acquainted with the
business, and by my father's instructions and the general
growth of my own powers, I was in a few years qualified
to be, and practically was, the chief conductor of the correspondence with India in one of the leading departments, that of the Native States. This continued to be my
official duty until I was appointed Examiner, only two
years before the time when the abolition of the East India
Company as a political body determined my retirement.
I do not know any one of the occupations, by which a
subsistence can now be gained, more suitable than such
as this to any one who, not being in independent circumstances, desires to devote a part of the twenty-four
hours to private intellectual pursuits. Writing for the
press cannot be recommended as a permanent resource
to any one qualified to accomplish anything in the higher
departments of literature or thought: not only on account
of the uncertainty of this means of livelihood, especially
if the writer has a conscience, and will not consent to
serve any opinions except his own; but also because the
writings by which one can live are not the writings
which themselves live, and are never those in which the
writer does his best. Books destined to form future thinkers take too much time to write, and when written come,
in general, too slowly into notice and repute to be relied
on for subsistence. Those who have to support themselves
by their pen must depend on literary drudgery, or at best
on writings addressed to the multitude; and can employ
in the pursuits of their own choice only such time as

they can spare from those of necessity; which is generally less than the leisure allowed by office occupations, while the effect on the mind is far more enervating and fatiguing. For my own part I have, through life, found office duties an actual rest from the other mental occupations which I have carried on simultaneously with them. They were sufficiently intellectual not to be a distasteful drudgery, without being such as to cause any strain upon the mental powers of a person used to abstract thought, or to the labour of careful literary composition. The drawbacks, for every mode of life has its drawbacks, were not, however, unfelt by me. I cared little for the loss of the chances of riches and honours held out by some of the professions, particularly the bar, which had been, as I have already said, the profession thought of for me. But I was not indifferent to exclusion from Parliament, and public life; and I felt very sensibly the more immediate unpleasantness of confinement to London; the holiday allowed by India-House practice not exceeding a month in the year, while my taste was strong for a country life, and my sojourn in France had left behind it an ardent desire of travelling. But though these tastes could not be freely indulged, they were at no time entirely sacrificed. I passed most Sundays, throughout the year, in the country, taking long rural walks on that day even when residing in London. The month's holiday was, for a few years, passed at my father's house in the country; afterwards a part or the whole was spent in tours, chiefly pedestrian, with some one or more of the young men who were my chosen companions; and, at a later period, in longer journeys or excursions, alone or with other friends. France, Belgium, and Rhenish Germany were within easy reach of the annual holiday; and two longer absences, one of three, the other of six months, under medical advice, added Switzerland, the Tyrol, and Italy to my list. Fortunately, also, both these journeys occurred rather early, so as to give the benefit and charm of the remembrance to a large portion of life.

I am disposed to agree with what has been surmised by others, that the opportunity which my official position gave me of learning by personal observation the necessary conditions of the practical conduct of public affairs, has been of considerable value to me as a theoretical reformer of the opinions and institutions of my time. Not, indeed, that public business transacted on paper, to take effect on the other side of the globe, was of itself calculated to give much practical knowledge of life. But the occupation accustomed me to see and hear the difficulties of every course, and the means of obviating them, stated and discussed deliberately with a view to execution; it gave me opportunities of perceiving when public measures, and other political facts, did not produce the effects which had been expected of them, and from what causes; above all, it was valuable to me by making me, in this portion of my activity, merely one wheel in a machine, the whole of which had to work together. As a speculative writer, I should have had no one to consult but myself, and should have encountered in my speculations none of the obstacles which would have started up whenever they came to be applied to practice. But as a Secretary conducting political correspondence, I could not issue an order or express an opinion, without satisfying various persons very unlike myself that the thing was fit to be done. I was thus in a good position for finding out by practice the mode of putting a thought which gives it easiest admittance into minds not prepared for it by habit; while I became practically conversant with the difficulties of moving bodies of men, the necessities of compromise, the art of sacrificing the non-essential to preserve the essential. I learnt how to obtain the best I could when I could not obtain everything; instead of being indignant or dispirited because I could not have entirely my own way, to be pleased and encouraged when I could have the smallest part of it; and when even that could not be, to bear with complete equanimity the being overruled altogether. I have found, through life, these acquisitions to be of the greatest possible importance for personal happiness, and they are also a very necessary condition for enabling any one, either as theorist or as practical man, to effect the greatest amount of good compatible with his opportunities.

CHAPTER IV   1823-1828

YOUTHFUL PROPAGANDISM; *West-minster Review*

The occupation of so much of my time by office work did not relax my attention to my own pursuits, which were never carried on more vigorously. It was about this time that I began to write in newspapers. The first writings of mine which got into print were two letters published towards the end of 1822, in the *Traveller* evening newspaper. The *Traveller* (which afterwards grew into the *Globe and Traveller,* by the purchase and incorporation of the *Globe*) was then the property of the well-known political economist, Colonel Torrens, and under the editorship of an able man, Mr. Walter Coulson (who, after being an amanuensis of Mr. Bentham, became a reporter, then an editor, next a barrister and conveyancer, and died Counsel to the Home Office), it had become one of the most important newspaper organs of Liberal politics. Colonel Torrens himself wrote much of the

political economy of his paper; and had at this time
made an attack upon some opinion of Ricardo and my
father, to which, at my father's instigation, I attempted an
answer, and Coulson, out of consideration for my father
and goodwill to me, inserted it. There was a reply by
Torrens, to which I again rejoined. I soon after attempted
something considerably more ambitious. The prosecutions
of Richard Carlile and his wife and sister, for publications
hostile to Christianity, were then exciting much attention,
and nowhere more than among the people I frequented.
Freedom of discussion even in politics, much more in religion, was at that time far from being, even in theory,
the conceded point which it at least seems to be now;
and the holders of obnoxious opinions had to be always
ready to argue and re-argue for the liberty of expressing
them. I wrote a series of five letters, under the signature
of Wickliffe, going over the whole length and breadth of
the question of free publication of all opinions on religion,
and offered them to the *Morning Chronicle*. Three of them
were published in January and February, 1823; the other
two, containing things too outspoken for that journal,
never appeared at all. But a paper which I wrote soon after
on the same subject, *à propos* of a debate in the House
of Commons, was inserted as a leading article; and during
the whole of this year, 1823, a considerable number of
my contributions were printed in the *Chronicle* and
Traveller: sometimes notices of books but often letters
commenting on some nonsense talked in Parliament, or
some defect of the law, or misdoings of the magistracy or
the courts of justice. In this last department the *Chronicle*
was now rendering signal service. After the death of Mr.
Perry, the editorship and management of the paper had
devolved on Mr. John Black, long a reporter on its
establishment; a man of most extensive reading and information, great honesty and simplicity of mind; a particular friend of my father, imbued with many of his and
Bentham's ideas, which he reproduced in his articles,
among other valuable thoughts, with great facility and
skill. From this time the *Chronicle* ceased to be the merely
Whig organ it was before, and during the next ten years
became to a considerable extent a vehicle of the opinions
of the Utilitarian Radicals. This was mainly by what Black
himself wrote, with some assistance from Fonblanque,

who first showed his eminent qualities as a writer by articles and *jeux d'esprit* in the *Chronicle*. The defects of the law, and of the administration of justice, were the subject on which that paper rendered most service to improvement. Up to that time hardly a word had been said, except by Bentham and my father, against that most peccant part of English institutions and of their administration. It was the almost universal creed of Englishmen that the law of England, the judicature of England, the unpaid magistracy of England, were models of excellence. I do not go beyond the mark in saying that after Bentham, who supplied the principal materials, the greatest share of the merit of breaking down this wretched superstition belongs to Black, as editor of the *Morning Chronicle*. He kept up an incessant fire against it, exposing the absurdities and vices of the law and the courts of justice, paid and unpaid, until he forced some sense of them into people's minds. On many other questions he became the organ of opinions much in advance of any which had ever before found regular advocacy in the newspaper press. Black was a frequent visitor of my father, and Mr. Grote used to say that he always knew, by the Monday morning's article, whether Black had been with my father on the Sunday. Black was one of the most influential of the many channels through which my father's conversation and personal influence made his opinions tell on the world; co-operating with the effect of his writings in making him a power in the country, such as it has rarely been the lot of an individual in a private station to be, through the mere force of intellect and character; and a power which was often acting the most efficiently where it was least seen and suspected. I have already noticed how much of what was done by Ricardo, Hume, and Grote, was the result, in part, of his prompting and persuasion. He was the good genius by the side of Brougham in most of what he did for the public, either on education, law reform, or any other subject. And his influence flowed in minor streams too numerous to be specified. This influence was now about to receive a great extension by the foundation of the *Westminister Review*.

Contrary to what may have been supposed, my father was in no degree a party to setting up the *Westminister Review*. The need of a Radical organ to make head

against the *Edinburgh* and *Quarterly* (then in the period
of their greatest reputation and influence), had been a
topic of conversation between him and Mr. Bentham many
years earlier, and it had been a part of their *Château en
Espagne* that my father should be the editor; but the
idea had never assumed any practical shape. In 1823,
however, Mr. Bentham determined to establish the *Review*
at his own cost, and offered the editorship to my father,
who declined it as incompatible with his India-House
appointment. It was then entrusted to Mr. (now Sir John)
Bowring, at that time a merchant in the city. Mr. Bowring
had been for two or three years previous an assiduous
frequenter of Mr. Bentham, to whom he was recommended
by many personal good qualities, by an ardent admiration
for Bentham, a zealous adoption of many, though not
all of his opinions, and, not least, by an extensive acquaint-
anceship and correspondence with Liberals of all countries,
which seemed to qualify him for being a powerful agent
in spreading Bentham's fame and doctrines through all
quarters of the world. My father had seen little of Bowring, but knew enough of him to have formed a strong
opinion that he was a man of an entirely different
type from what my father considered suitable for conducting a political and philosophical *Review*: and he augured
so ill of enterprise that he regretted it altogether, feeling
persuaded not only that Mr. Bentham would lose his
money, but that discredit would probably be brought upon
Radical principles. He could not, however, desert Mr.
Bentham, and he consented to write an article for the
first number. As it had been a favourite portion of the
scheme formerly talked of that part of the work should
be devoted to reviewing the other *Reviews,* this article of
my father's was to be a general criticism of the *Edinburgh
Review* from its commencement. Before writing it he made
me read through all the volumes of the *Review,* or as much
of each as seemed of any importance (which was not so
arduous a task in 1823 as it would be now), and make
notes for him of the articles which I thought he would
wish to examine, either on account of their good or their
bad qualities. This paper of my father's was the chief
cause of the sensation which the *Westminister Review*
produced at its first appearance, and is, both in conception
and in execution, one of the most striking of all his writ-

ings. He began by an analysis of the tendencies of periodical literature in general; pointing out, that it cannot, like books, wait for success, but must succeed immediately, or not at all, and is hence almost certain to profess and inculcate the opinions already held by the public to which it addresses itself, instead of attempting to rectify or improve those opinions. He next, to characterize the position of the *Edinburgh Review* as a political organ, entered into a complete analysis, from the Radical point of view, of the British Constitution. He held up to notice its thoroughly aristocratic character: the nomination of a majority of the House of Commons by a few hundred families; the entire identification of the more independent portion, the county members, with the great landholders; the different classes whom this narrow oligarchy was induced, for convenience, to admit to a share of power; and finally, what he called its two props, the Church, and the legal profession. He pointed out the natural tendency of an aristocratic body of this composition, to group itself into two parties, one of them in possession of the executive, the other endeavoring to supplant the former and become the predominant section by the aid of public opinion, without any essential sacrifice of the aristocratical predominance. He described the course likely to be pursued, and the political ground occupied, by an aristocratic party in opposition, coquetting with popular principles for the sake of popular support. He showed how this idea was realized in the conduct of the Whig party, and of the *Edinburgh Review* as its chief literary organ. He described, as their main characteristic, what he termed "seesaw"; writing alternately on both sides of every question which touched the power or interest of the governing classes; sometimes in different articles, sometimes in different parts of the same article; and illustrated his position by copious specimens. So formidable an attack on the Whig party and policy had never before been made; nor had so great a blow been ever struck, in this country, for radicalism; nor was there, I believe, any living person capable of writing that article, except my father.*

* The continuation of this article in the second number of the *Review* was written by me under my father's eye, and (except as practice in composition, in which respect it was, to me, more useful than anything else I ever wrote) was of little or no value.

In the meantime the nascent *Review* had formed a junction with another project of a purely literary periodical to be edited by Mr. Henry Southern, afterwards a diplomatist, then a literary man by profession. The two editors agreed to unite their corps, and divide the editorship, Bowring taking the political, Southern the literary department. Southern's *Review* was to have been published by Longman, and that firm, though part proprietors of the *Edinburgh,* were willing to be the publishers of the new journal. But when all the arrangements had been made, and the prospectus sent out, the Longmans saw my father's attack on the *Edinburgh,* and drew back. My father was now appealed to for his interest with his own publisher, Baldwin, which was exerted with a successful result. And so, in April, 1824, amidst anything but hope on my father's part, and that of most of those who afterwards aided in carrying on the *Review,* the first number made its appearance.

That number was an agreeable surprise to most of us. The average of the articles was of much better quality than had been expected. The literary and artistic department had rested chiefly on Mr. Bingham, a barrister (subsequently a police magistrate), who had been for some years a frequenter of Bentham, was a friend of both the Austins, and had adopted with great ardour Mr. Bentham's philosophical opinions. Partly from accident, there were in the first number as many as five articles by Bingham; and we were extremely pleased with them. I well remember the mixed feeling I myself had about the *Review;* the joy at finding what we did not at all expect, that it was sufficiently good to be capable of being made a creditable organ of those who held the opinions it professed; and extreme vexation, since it was so good on the whole, at what we thought the blemishes of it. When, however, in addition to our generally favourable opinion of it, we learned that it had an extraordinary large sale for a first number, and found that the appearance of a Radical review, with pretentions equal to those of the established organs of parties, had excited much attention, there could be no room for hesitation, and we all became eager in doing everything we could to strengthen and improve it.

My father continued to write occasional articles. The

Quarterly Review received its exposure, as a sequel to that of the *Edinburgh.* Of his other contributions, the most important were an attack on Southey's *Book of the Church,* in the fifth number, and a political article in the twelfth. Mr. Austin only contributed one paper, but one of great merit, an argument against primogeniture, in reply to an article then lately published in the *Edinburgh Review* by McCulloch. Grote also was a contributor only once; all the time he could spare being already taken up with his *History of Greece.* The article he wrote was on his own subject, and was a very complete exposure and castigation of Mitford. Bingham and Charles Austin continued to write for some time; Fonblanque was a frequent contributor from the third number. Of my particular associates, Ellis was a regular writer up to the ninth number; and about the time when he left off, others of the set began; Eyton Tooke, Graham, and Roebuck. I was myself the most frequent writer of all, having contributed, from the second number to the eighteenth, thirteen articles; reviews of books on history and political economy, or discussions on special political topics, as corn laws, game laws, law of libel. Occasional articles of merit came in from other acquaintances of my father's, and, in time, of mine; and some of Mr. Bowring's writers turned out well. On the whole, however, the conduct of the *Review* was never satisfactory to any of the persons strongly interested in its principles, with whom I came in contact. Hardly ever did a number come out without containing several things extremely offensive to us, either in point of opinion, of taste, or by mere want of ability. The unfavourable judgments passed by my father, Grote, the two Austins, and others, were re-echoed with exaggeration by us younger people; and as our youthful zeal rendered us by no means backward in making complaints, we led the two editors a sad life. From my knowledge of what I then was, I have no doubt that we were at least as often wrong as right; and I am very certain that if the *Review* had been carried on according to our notions (I mean those of the juniors), it would have been no better, perhaps not even so good as it was. But it is worth noting as a fact in the history of Benthamism that the periodical organ by which it was best known was from the first extremely unsatisfactory to those whose opinions on all subjects it was supposed specifically to represent.

Meanwhile, however, the *Review* made considerable noise in the world, and gave a recognised status, in the arena of opinion and discussion, to the Benthamic type of radicalism, out of all proportion to the number of its adherents, and to the personal merits and abilities, at that time, of most of those who could be reckoned among them. It was a time, as is known, of rapidly rising liberalism. When the fears and animosities accompanying the war with France had been brought to an end, and people had once more a place in their thoughts for home politics, the tide began to set towards reform. The renewed oppression of the Continent by the old reigning families, the countenance apparently given by the English government to the conspiracy against liberty called the Holy Alliance, and the enormous weight of the national debt and taxation occasioned by so long and costly a war, rendered the government and Parliament very unpopular. Radicalism, under the leadership of the Burdetts and Cobbetts, had assumed a character and importance which seriously alarmed the Administration; and their alarm had scarcely been temporarily assuaged by the celebrated Six Acts, when the trial of Queen Caroline roused a still wider and deeper feeling of hatred. Though the outward signs of this hatred passed away with its exciting cause, there arose on all sides a spirit which had never shown itself before, of opposition to abuses in detail. Mr. Hume's persevering scrutiny of the public expenditure, forcing the House of Commons to a division on every objectionable item in the estimates, has begun to tell with great force on public opinion, and had extorted many minor retrenchments from an unwilling administration. Political economy had asserted itself with great vigour in public affairs by the petition of the merchants of London for free trade, drawn up in 1820 by Mr. Tooke and presented by Mr. Alexander Baring; and by the noble exertions of Ricardo during the few years of his parliamentary life. His writings, following up the impulse given by the bullion controversy, and followed up in their turn by the expositions and comments of my father and McCulloch (whose writings in the *Edinburgh Review* during those years were most valuable), had drawn gener-

al attention to the subject, making at least partial converts in the Cabinet itself; and Huskisson, supported by
Canning, had commenced that gradual demolition of the
protective system, which one of their colleagues virtually
completed in 1846, though the last vestiges were only
swept away by Mr. Gladstone in 1860. Mr. Peel, then
Home Secretary, was entering cautiously into the un-
trodden and peculiarly Benthamic path of law reform. At
this period, when Liberalism seemed to be becoming the
tone of the time, when improvement of institutions was
preached from the highest places, and a complete change
of the constitution of Parliament was loudly demanded in
the lowest, it is not strange that attention should have
been roused by the regular appearance in controversy of
what seemed a new school of writers, claiming to be the
legislators and theorists of this new tendency. The air of
strong conviction with which they wrote, when scarcely
any one else seemed to have an equally strong faith in as
definite a creed; the boldness with which they tilted against
the very front of both the existing political parties; their
uncompromising profession of opposition to many of the
generally received opinions, and the suspicion they lay
under of holding others still more heterodox than they
professed; the talent and verve of at least my father's articles, and the appearance of a corps behind him sufficient
to carry on a *Review*; and, finally, the fact that the *Review*
was bought and read, made the so-called Bentham school
in philosophy and politics fill a greater place in the public
mind than it had held before, or has ever again held since
other equally earnest schools of thought have arisen in
England. As I was in the head-quarters of it, knew of
what it was composed, and as one of the most active of
its very small number might say without undue assump-
tion, *quorum pars magna fui*, it belongs to me more
than to most others to give some account of it.

This supposed school, then, had no other existence
than what was constituted by the fact that my father's
writings and conversation drew round him a certain number of young men who had already imbibed, or who imbibed from him, a greater or smaller portion of his very
decided political and philosophical opinions. The notion
that Bentham was surrounded by a band of disciples who
received their opinions from his lips is a fable to which my

father did justice in his *Fragment on Mackintosh,* and which, to all who knew Mr. Bentham's habits of life and manner of conversation, is simply ridiculous. The influence which Bentham exercised was by his writings. Through them he had produced, and is producing, effects on the condition of mankind, wider and deeper, no doubt, than any which can be attributed to my father. He is a much greater name in history. But my father exercised a far greater personal ascendancy. He *was* sought for the vigour and instructiveness of his conversation, and did use it largely as an instrument for the diffusion of his opinions. I have never known any man who could do such ample justice to his best thoughts in colloquial discussion. His perfect command over his great mental resources, the terseness and expressiveness of his language and the moral earnestness as well as intellectual force of his delivery, made him one of the most striking of all argumentative conversers; and he was full of anecdote, a hearty laugher, and, when with people whom he liked, a most lively and amusing companion. It was not solely, or even chiefly, in diffusing his merely intellectual convictions that his power showed itself; it was still more through the influence of a quality, of which I have only since learnt to appreciate the extreme rarity: that exalted public spirit, and regard above all things to the good of the whole, which warmed into life and activity every germ of similar virtue that existed in the minds he came in contact with; the desire he made them feel for his approbation, the shame at his disapproval; the moral support which his conversation and his very existence gave to those who were aiming at the same objects, and the encouragement he afforded to the faint-hearted or desponding among them by the firm confidence which (though the reverse of sanguine as to the results to be expected in any one particular case), he always felt in the power of reason, the general progress of improvement, and the good which individuals could do by judicious effort.

It was my father's opinions which gave the distinguishing character to the Benthamic or Utilitarian propagandism of that time. They fell singly, scattered from him, in many directions, but they flowed from him in a continued stream principally in three channels. One was through me, the only mind directly formed by his instructions, and through whom considerable influence was exercised over various young men, who became, in their turn, propagandists. A second was through some of the Cambridge contemporaries of Charles Austin, who, either initiated by him or under the general mental impulse which he gave, had adopted many opinions allied to those of my father, and some of the more considerable of whom afterwards sought my father's acquaintance and frequented his house. Among these may be mentioned Strutt, afterwards Lord Belper, and the present Lord Romilly, with whose eminent father, Sir Samuel, my father had of old been on terms of friendship. The third channel was that of a younger generation of Cambridge undergraduates, contemporary not with Austin, but with Eyton Tooke, who were drawn to that estimable person by affinity of opinions, and introduced by him to my father: the most notable of these was Charles Buller. Various other persons individually received and transmitted a considerable amount of my father's influence: for example, Black (as before mentioned) and Fonblanque; most of these, however, we accounted only partial allies; Fonblanque, for instance, was always divergent from us on many important points. But indeed there was by no means complete unanimity among any portion of us, nor had any of us adopted implicitly all my father's opinions. For example, although his *Essay on Government* was regarded probably by all of us as a masterpiece of political wisdom, our adhesion by no means extended to the paragraph of it, in which he maintains that women may consistently with good government be excluded from the suffrage, because their interest is the same with that of men. From this doctrine, I, and all those who formed my chosen associates, most positively dissented. It is due to my father to say that he denied having intended to affirm that women *should* be excluded, any more than men under the age of forty, concerning whom he maintained, in the very next paragraph, an exactly similar thesis. He was, as he truly said, not discussing whether the suffrage had better be restricted, but only (assuming that it is to be restricted) what is the utmost limit of restriction, which does not necessarily involve a sacrifice of the securities for good government. But I thought then, as I have always thought since, that the opinion which he acknowledged, no less than that which he disclaimed, is as great an error as any of those against which the *Essay* was directed; that the interest of women is included in that of men exactly as much and no more as the interest of subjects is included in that of kings; and that every reason which exists for giving the suffrage to anybody demands that it should not be withheld from women. This was also the general opinion of the younger proselytes; and it is pleasant to be able to say that Mr. Bentham, on this important point, was wholly on our side.

But though none of us, probably, agreed in every respect with my father, his opinions, as I said before, were the principal element which gave its colour and character to the little group of young men who were the first propagators of what was afterwards called "philosophic Radicalism." Their mode of thinking was not characterized by Benthamism in any sense which has relation to Bentham as a chief or guide but rather by a combination of Bentham's point of view with that of the modern political economy, and with the Hartleian metaphysics. Malthus' population principle was quite as much a banner, and point of union among us, as any opinion specially belonging to Bentham. This great doctrine, originally brought forward as an argument against the indefinite improvability of human affairs, we took up with ardent zeal in the contrary sense, as indicating the sole means of realizing that improvability by securing full employment at high wages to the whole labouring population through a voluntary restriction of the increase of their numbers. The other leading characteristics of the creed, which we held in common with my father, may be stated as follows:

In politics, an almost unbounded confidence in the efficacy of two things: representative government, and complete freedom of discussion. So complete was my father's reliance on the influence of reason over the minds of mankind, whenever it is allowed to reach them, that he felt as if all would be gained if the whole population were taught to read, if all sorts of opinions were allowed to be addressed to them by word and in writing, and if by means of the suffrage they could nominate a legislature to give effect to the opinions they adopted. He thought that when the legislature no longer represented a class interest, it would aim at the general interest,

honestly and with adequate wisdom; since the people
would be sufficiently under the guidance of educated intelligence to make in general a good choice of persons
to represent them, and having done so, to leave to those
whom they had chosen a liberal discretion. Accordingly,
aristocratic rule, the government of the few in any of its
shapes, being in his eyes the only thing which stood between mankind and an administration of their affairs by
the best wisdom to be found among them, was the object
of his sternest disapprobation, and a democratic suffrage
the principal article of his political creed, not on the
ground of liberty, Rights of Man, or any of the phrases,
more or less significant, by which, up to that time, democracy had usually been defended, but as the most essential of "securities for good government." In this, too,
he held fast only to what he deemed essentials; he was
comparatively indifferent to monarchical or republican
forms—far more so than Bentham, to whom a king, in
the character of "corrupter-general," appeared necessarily
very noxious. Next to aristocracy, an established church,
or corporation of priests, as being by position the great
depravers of religion, and interested in opposing the
progress of the human mind, was the object of his greatest
detestation; though he disliked no clergyman personally
who did not deserve it, and was on terms of sincere friendship with several. In ethics, his moral feelings were
energetic and rigid on all points which he deemed important to human well-being, while he was supremely
indifferent in opinion (though his indifference did not
show itself in personal conduct) to all those doctrines of
the common morality which he thought had no foundation
but in asceticism and priestcraft. He looked forward, for
example, to a considerable increase of freedom in the relations between the sexes, though without pretending to
define exactly what would be, or ought to be, the precise
conditions of that freedom. This opinion was connected in
him with no sensuality either of a theatrical or of a practical kind. He anticipated, on the contrary, as one of the
beneficial effects of increased freedom, that the imagination
would no longer dwell upon the physical relation and its
adjuncts, and swell this into one of the principal objects of life; a perversion of the imagination and feelings,
which he regarded as one of the deepest seated and most

pervading evils in the human mind. In psychology, his fundamental doctrine was the formation of all human character by circumstances, through the universal principle of association, and the consequent unlimited possibility of improving the moral and intellectual condition of mankind by education. Of all his doctrines none was more important than this, or needs more to be insisted on; unfortunately there is none which is more contradictory to the prevailing tendencies of speculation, both in his time and since.

These various opinions were seized on with youthful fanaticism by the little knot of young men of whom I was one; and we put into them a sectarian spirit, from which, in intention at least, my father was wholly free. What we (or rather a phantom substituted in the place of us) were sometimes by ridiculous exaggeration called by others, namely a "school," some of us for a time really hoped and aspired to be. The French *philosophes* of the eighteenth century were the example we sought to imitate, and we hoped to accomplish no less results. No one of the set went to so great excesses in this boyish ambition as I did; which might be shown by many particulars, were it not an useless waste of space and time.

All this, however, is properly only the outside of our existence; or, at least, the intellectual part alone, and no more than one side of that. In attempting to penetrate inward, and give any indication of what we were as human beings, I must be understood as speaking only of myself, of whom alone I can speak from sufficient knowledge; and I do not believe that the picture would suit any of my companions without many and great modifications.

I conceive that the description so often given of a Benthamite as a mere reasoning machine, though extremely inapplicable to most of those who have been designated by that title, was during two or three years of my life not altogether untrue of me. It was perhaps as applicable to me as it can well be to any one just entering into life, to whom the common objects of desire must in general have at least the attraction of novelty. There is nothing very extraordinary in this fact: no youth of the age I then was can be expected to be more than one thing, and this was the thing I happened to be. Ambition and desire of distinction I had in abundance; and zeal for what I thought the good of mankind was my strongest sentiment, mixing with and colouring all others. But my zeal was as yet little else, at that period of my life, than zeal for speculative opinions. It had not its root in genuine benevolence, or sympathy with mankind; though these qualities held their due place in my ethical standard. Nor was it connected with any high enthusiasm for ideal nobleness. Yet of this feeling I was imaginatively very susceptible; but there was at that time an intermission of its natural aliment, poetical culture, while there was a superabundance of the discipline antagonistic to it, that of mere logic and analysis. Add to this that, as already mentioned, my father's teachings tended to the undervaluing of feeling. It was not that he was himself cold-hearted or insensible; I believe it was rather from the contrary quality; he thought that feeling could take care of itself; that there was sure to be enough of it if actions were properly cared about. Offended by the frequency with which, in ethical and philosophical controversy, feeling is made the ultimate reason and justification of conduct instead of being itself called on for a justification, while, in practice, actions the effect of which on human happiness is mischievous are defended as being required by feeling, and the character of a person of feeling obtains a credit for desert, which he thought only due to actions, he had a real impatience of attributing praise to feeling, or of any but the most sparing reference to it, either in the estimation of persons or in the discussion of things. In addition to the influence which this characteristic in him had on me and others, we found all the opinions to which we attached most importance constantly attacked on the ground of feeling. Utility was denounced as cold calculation; political economy as hard-hearted; anti-population doctrines as repulsive to the natural feelings of mankind. We retorted by the word "sentimentality," which, along with "declamation" and "vague generalities," served us as common terms of opprobrium. Although we were generally in the right, as against those who were opposed to us, the effect was that the cultivation of feeling (except the feelings of public and private duty), was not in much esteem among us, and had very little place in the thoughts of most of us, myself in particular. What we principally thought of was to alter people's opinions; to make them believe according to evidence, and know what was their real interest, which when they once knew, they would, we thought, by the instrument of opinion, enforce a regard to it upon one another. While fully recognizing the superior excellence of unselfish benevolence and love of justice, we did not expect the regeneration of mankind from any direct action on those sentiments, but from the effect of educated intellect, enlightening the selfish feelings. Although this last is prodigiously important as a means of improvement in the hands of those who are themselves impelled by nobler principles of action, I do not believe that any one of the survivors of the Benthamites or Utilitarians of that day now relies mainly upon it for the general amendment of human conduct.

From this neglect both in theory and in practice of the cultivation of feeling, naturally resulted, among other things, an undervaluing of poetry, and of imagination generally, as an element of human nature. It is, or was, part of the popular notion of Benthamites that they are enemies of poetry; this was partly true of Bentham himself: he used to say that "all poetry is misrepresentation"; but in the sense in which he said it, the same might have been said of all impressive speech; of all representation or inculcation more oratorical in its character than a sum in arithmetic. An article of Bingham's in the first number of the *Westminster Review*, in which he offered as an explanation of something which he disliked in Moore, that "Mr. Moore *is* a poet, and therefore is *not* a reasoner," did a good deal to attach the notion of hating poetry to the writers in the *Review*. But the truth was that many of us were great readers of poetry; Bingham himself had been a writer of it, while as regards me (and the same thing might be said of my father), the correct statement would be, not that I disliked poetry, but that I was theoretically indifferent to it. I disliked any sentiments in poetry which I should have disliked in prose; and that included a great deal. And I was wholly blind to its place in human culture as a means of educating the feelings. But I was always personally very susceptible to some kinds of it. In the most sectarian period of my Benthamism, I happened to look into Pope's *Essay on Man*, and though every opinion in it was contrary to mine, I well remember how powerfully it acted on my imagination. Perhaps at that time poetical composition of any higher type than eloquent discussion in verse might not have produced a similar effect on me; at all events I seldom gave it an opportunity. This, however, was a mere passive state. Long before I had enlarged, in any considerable degree, the basis of my intellectual creed, I had obtained in the natural course of my mental progress, poetic culture of the most valuable kind, by means of reverential admiration for the lives and characters of heroic persons; especially the heroes of philosophy. The same inspiring effect which so many of the benefactors of mankind have left on record that they had experienced from *Plutarch's Lives*, was produced on me by Plato's pictures of Socrates, and by some modern biographies, above all by Condorcet's *Life of Turgot*; a book well calculated to rouse the best sort of enthusiasm, since it contains one of the wisest and noblest of lives, delineated by one of the wisest and noblest of men. The heroic virtue of these glorious representatives of the opinions with which I sympathized deeply affected me, and I perpetually recurred to them as others do to a favourite poet, when needing to be carried up into the more elevated regions of feeling and thought. I may observe by the way that this book cured me of my sectarian follies. The two or three pages beginning "Il regardait toute secte comme nuisible," and explaining why Turgot always kept himself perfectly distinct from the Encyclopædists, sank deeply into my mind. I left off designating myself and others as Utilitarians, and by the pronoun "we" or any other collective designation, I ceased to *afficher* sectarianism. My real inward sectarianism I did not get rid of till later, and much more gradually.

About the end of 1824, or beginning of 1825, Mr. Bentham, having lately got back his papers on *Evidence* from M. Dumont (whose *Traité des Preuves Judiciaires*, grounded on them, was then first completed and published) resolved to have them printed in the original, and bethought himself of me as capable of preparing them for the press; in the same manner as his *Book of Fallacies* had been recently edited by Bingham. I gladly undertook this task, and it occupied nearly all my leisure for about a year, exclusive of the time afterwards spent in seeing the five large volumes through the press. Mr. Bentham had begun this treatise three times, at considerable intervals, each time in a different manner, and each time without reference to the preceding; two of the three times he had gone over nearly the whole subject. These three masses of manuscript it was my business to condense into a single treatise; adopting the one last written as the groundwork, and incorporating with it as much of the two others as it had not completely superseded. I had also to unroll such of Bentham's involved and parenthetical sentences as seemed to overpass by their complexity the measure of what readers were likely to take the pains to understand. It was further Mr. Bentham's particular desire that I should, from myself, endeavour to supply any lacunæ which he had left; and at his instance I read, for this purpose, the most authoritative treatises on the English law of evidence, and commented on a few of the objectionable points of the English rules, which had escaped Bentham's notice. I also replied to the objections which had been made to some of his doctrines by reviewers of Dumont's book, and added a few supplementary remarks on some of the more abstract parts of the subject, such as the theory of improbability and impossibility. The controversial part of these editorial additions was written in a more assuming tone than became one so young and inexperienced as I was; but indeed I had never contemplated coming forward in my own person; and as an anonymous editor of Bentham, I fell into the tone of my author, not thinking it unsuitable to him or to the subject, however it might be so to me. My name as editor was put to the book after it was printed, at Mr. Bentham's positive desire, which I in vain attempted to persuade him to forego.

The time occupied in this editorial work was extremely well employed in respect to my own improvement. The *Rationale of Judicial Evidence* is one of the richest in matter of all Bentham's productions. The theory of evidence being in itself one of the most important of his subjects, and ramifying into most of the others, the book contains, very fully developed, a great proportion of all his best thoughts: while, among more special things, it comprises the most elaborate exposure of the vices and defects of English law, as it then was, which is to be found in his works; not confined to the law of evidence, but including, by way of illustrative episode, the entire procedure or practice of Westminster Hall. The direct knowledge, therefore, which I obtained from the book, and which was imprinted upon me much more thoroughly than it could have been by mere reading, was itself no small acquisition. But this occupation did for me what might seem less to be expected; it gave a great start to my powers of composition. Everything which I wrote subsequently to this editorial employment was markedly superior to anything that I had written before it. Bentham's later style, as the world knows, was heavy and cumbersome, from the excess of a good quality, the love of precision, which made him introduce clause within clause into the heart of every sentence, that the reader might receive into his mind all the modifications and qualifications simultaneously with the main proposition; and the habit grew on him until his sentences became, to those not accustomed to them, most laborious reading. But his earlier style, that of the *Fragment on Government, Plan of a Judicial Establishment*, etc., is a model of liveliness and ease combined with fullness of matter, scarcely ever surpassed; and of this earlier style there were many striking specimens in the manuscripts on *Evidence*, all of which I endeavoured to preserve. So long a course of this admirable writing had a considerable effect upon my own; and I added to it by the assiduous reading of other writers, both French and English, who combined, in a remarkable degree, ease with force, such as Goldsmith, Fielding, Pascal, Voltaire, and Courier. Through these influences my writing lost the jejuneness of my early compositions; the bones and cartilages began to clothe themselves with flesh, and the style became, at times, lively and almost light.

This improvement was first exhibited in a new field. Mr. Marshall, of Leeds, father of the present generation of Marshalls, the same who was brought into Parliament for Yorkshire, when the representation forfeited by Grampound was transferred to it, an earnest parliamentary reformer, and a man of large fortune, of which he made a liberal use, had been much struck with Bentham's *Book of Fallacies*; and the thought had occurred to him that it would be useful to publish annually the *Parliamentary*

Debates, not in the chronological order of Hansard, but classified according to subjects, and accompanied by a commentary pointing out the fallacies of the speakers. With this intention, he very naturally addressed himself to the editor of the *Book of Fallacies*; and Bingham, with the assistance of Charles Austin, undertook the editorship. The work was called *Parliamentary History and Review.* Its sale was not sufficient to keep it in existence, and it only lasted three years. It excited, however, some attention among parliamentary and political people. The best strength of the party was put forth in it; and its execution did them much more credit than that of the *Westminster Review* had ever done. Bingham and Charles Austin wrote much in it; as did Strutt, Romilly, and several other Liberal lawyers. My father wrote one article in his best style; the elder Austin another. Coulson wrote one of great merit. It fell to my lot to lead off the first number by an article on the principal topic of the session (that of 1825), "The Catholic Association and the Catholic Disabilities." In the second number I wrote an elaborate "Essay on the Commercial Crisis of 1825 and the Currency Debates." In the third I had two articles, one on a minor subject, the other on the reciprocity principle in commerce, *à propos* of a celebrated diplomatic correspondence between Canning and Gallatin. These writings were no longer mere reproductions and applications of the doctrines I had been taught: they were original thinking, as far as that name can be applied to old ideas in new forms and connexions; and I do not exceed the truth in saying that there was a maturity, and a well-digested character about them, which there had not been in any of my previous performances. In execution, therefore, they were not at all juvenile; but their subjects have either gone by, or have been so much better treated since, that they are entirely superseded, and should remain buried in the same oblivion with my contributions to the first dynasty of the *Westminster Review.*

While thus engaged in writing for the public, I did not neglect other modes of self-cultivation. It was at this time that I learnt German; beginning it on the Hamiltonian method, for which purpose I and several of my companions formed a class. For several years from this period, our social studies assumed a shape which contributed very much to my mental progress. The idea occurred to us of carrying on, by reading and conversation, a joint study of several of the branches of science which we wished to be masters of. We assembled to the number of a dozen or more. Mr. Grote lent a room of his house in Threadneedle Street for the purpose, and his partner, Prescott, one of the three original members of the Utilitarian Society, made one among us. We met two mornings in every week, from half-past eight till ten, at which hour most of us were called off to our daily occupations. Our first subject was political economy. We chose some systematic treatise as our text-book; my father's *Elements* being our first choice. One of us read aloud a chapter, or some smaller portion of the book. The discussion was then opened, and any one who had an objection, or other remark to make, made it. Our rule was to discuss thoroughly every point raised, whether great or small, prolonging the discussion until all who took part were satisfied with the conclusion they had individually arrived at; and to follow up every topic of collateral speculation which the chapter or the conversation suggested, never leaving it until we had untied every knot which we found. We repeatedly kept up the discussion of some one point for several weeks, thinking intently on it during the intervals of our meetings, and contriving solutions of the new difficulties which had risen up in the last morning's discussion. When we had finished in this way my father's *Elements*, we went in the same manner through Ricardo's *Principles of Political Economy,* and Bailey's *Dissertation on Value.* These close and vigorous discussions were not only improving in a high degree to those who took part in them, but brought out new views of some topics of abstract Political Economy. The theory of international values, which I afterwards published, emanated from these conversations, as did also the modified form of Ricardo's theory of profits, laid down in my *Essay on Profits and Interest.* Those among us with whom new speculations chiefly originated were Ellis, Graham, and I; though others gave valuable aid to the discussions, especially Prescott and Roebuck, the one by his knowledge, the other by his dialectical acuteness. The theories of inter-

national values and of profits were excogitated and worked
out in about equal proportions by myself and Graham;
and if our original project had been executed, my *Essays
on Some Unsettled Questions of Political Economy* would
have been brought out along with some papers, of his,
under our joint names. But when my exposition came
to be written, I found that I had so much over-estimated
my agreement with him, and he dissented so much from
the most original of the two *Essays*, that on international
values, that I was obliged to consider the theory as now
exclusively mine, and it came out as such when published many years later. I may mention that among the
alterations which my father made in revising his *Elements*
for the third edition, several were founded on criticisms
elicited by these conversations; and in particular he modified his opinions (though not to the extent of our new
speculations) on both the points to which I have adverted.

When we had enough of political economy, we took up
the syllogistic logic in the same manner, Grote now joining us. Our first text-book was Aldrich, but being dis-
gusted with its superficiality, we reprinted one of the most
finished among the many manuals of the school logic,
which my father, a great collector of such books, possessed, the *Manuductio ad Logicam* of the Jesuit Du
Trieu. After finishing this, we took up Whately's *Logic*,
then first republished from the *Encyclopaedia Metropo-
litana*, and finally the *Computatio sive Logica* of Hobbes.
These books, dealt with in our manner, afforded a wide
range for original metaphysical speculation; and most
of what has been done in the First Book of my *System of
Logic* to rationalize and correct the principles and distinctions of the school logicians, and to improve the theory
of the import of propositions, had its origin in these discussions; Graham and I originating most of the novelties,
while Grote and others furnished an excellent tribunal
or test. From this time I formed the project of writing a
book on *Logic,* though on a much humbler scale than
the one I ultimately executed.

Having done with logic, we launched into analytic
psychology, and having chosen Hartley for our textbook,
we raised Priestley's edition to an extravagant price by
searching through London to furnish each of us with a
copy. When we had finished Hartley, we suspended our

meetings; but my father's *Analysis of the Mind* being published soon after, we reassembled for the purpose of reading it. With this our exercises ended. I have always dated from these conversations my own real inauguration as an original and independent thinker. It was also through them that I acquired, or very much strengthened, a mental habit to which I attribute all that I have ever done, or ever shall do, in speculation: that of never accepting half-solutions of difficulties as complete; never abandoning a puzzle, but again and again returning to it until it was cleared up; never allowing obscure corners of a subject to remain unexplored because they did not appear important; never thinking that I perfectly understood any part of a subject until I understood the whole.

Our doings from 1825 to 1830 in the way of public speaking filled a considerable place in my life during those years, and as they had important effects on my development, something ought to be said of them.

There was for some time in existence a society of Owenites, called the Co-operation Society, which met for weekly public discussions in Chancery Lane. In the early part of 1825, accident brought Roebuck in contact with several of its members, and led to his attending one or two of the meetings and taking part in the debate in opposition to Owenism. Some one of us started the notion of going there in a body and having a general battle; and Charles Austin and some of his friends, who did not usually take part in our joint exercises, entered into the project. It was carried out by concert with the principal members of the Society, themselves nothing loth, as they naturally preferred a controversy with opponents to a tame discussion among their own body. The question of population was proposed as the subject of debate; Charles Austin led the case on our side with a brilliant speech, and the fight was kept up by adjournment through five or six weekly meetings before crowded auditories, including, along with the members of the Society and their friends, many hearers and some speakers from the Inns of Court. When this debate was ended, another was commenced on the general merits of Owen's system; and the contest altogether lasted about three months. It was a *lutte corps à corps* between Owenites and political economists, whom the Owenites regarded as their most inveterate opponents; but it was a perfectly friendly dispute. We, who represented political economy, had the same objects in view as they had, and took pains to show it; and the principal champion on their side was a very estimable man, with whom I was well acquainted, Mr. William Thompson, of Cork, author of a book on the *Distribution of Wealth*, and of an *Appeal* in behalf of women against the passage relating to them in my father's *Essay on Government*. Ellis, Roebuck, and I took an active part in the debate, and among those from the Inns of Court who joined in it, I remember Charles Villiers. The other side obtained also, on the population question, very efficient support from without. The well-known Gale Jones, then an elderly man, made one of his florid speeches; but the speaker with whom I was most struck, though I dissented from nearly every word he said, was Thirlwall, the historian, since Bishop of St. David's, then a Chancery barrister, unknown except by a high reputation for eloquence acquired at the Cambridge Union before the era of Austin and Macaulay. His speech was in answer to one of mine. Before he had uttered ten sentences, I set him down as the best speaker I had ever heard, and I have never since heard any one whom I placed above him.

The great interest of these debates predisposed some of those who took part in them to catch at a suggestion thrown out by McCulloch, the political economist, that a society was wanted in London similar to the Speculative Society at Edinburgh, in which Brougham, Horner, and others first cultivated public speaking. Our experience at the Co-operative Society seemed to give cause for being sanguine as to the sort of men who might be brought together in London for such a purpose. McCulloch mentioned the matter to several young men of influence, to whom he was then giving private lessons in political economy. Some of these entered warmly into the project, particularly George Villiers, afterwards Earl of Clarendon. He and his brothers, Hyde and Charles, Romilly, Charles Austin and I, with some others, met and agreed on a plan. We determined to meet once a fortnight from November to June, at the Freemasons' Tavern, and we had soon a fine list of members, containing, along with several members of Parliament, nearly all the most noted speak-

ers of the Cambridge Union and of the Oxford United
Debating Society. It is curiously illustrative of the tendencies of the time that our principal difficulty in re-
cruiting for the Society was to find a sufficient number
of Tory speakers. Almost all whom we could press into
the service were Liberals, of different orders and degrees.
Besides those already named, we had Macaulay, Thirlwall, Praed, Lord Howick, Samuel Wilberforce (afterwards Bishop of Oxford), Charles Poulett Thomson
(afterwards Lord Sydenham), Edward and Henry Lytton
Bulwer, Fonblanque, and many others whom I cannot
now recollect, but who made themselves afterwards more
or less conspicuous in public or literary life. Nothing
could seem more promising. But when the time for action
drew near, and it was necessary to fix on a president, and
find somebody to open the first debate, none of our
celebrities would consent to perform either office. Of the
many who were pressed on the subject, the only one who
could be prevailed on was a man of whom I knew very
little, but who had taken high honours at Oxford and
was said to have acquired a great oratorical reputation
there; who some time afterwards became a Tory member of Parliament. He accordingly was fixed on, both for
filling the President's chair and for making the first speech.
The important day arrived; the benches were crowded;
all our great speakers were present, to judge of, but not
to help our efforts. The Oxford orator's speech was a
complete failure. This threw a damp on the whole concern: the speakers who followed were few, and none of
them did their best; the affair was a complete fiasco; and
the oratorical celebrities we had counted on went away
never to return, giving to me at least a lesson in knowledge of the world. This unexpected break-down altered
my whole relation to the project. I had not anticipated
taking a prominent part, or speaking much or often, particularly at first, but I now saw that the success of the
scheme depended on the new men, and I put my shoulder
to the wheel. I opened the second question, and from
that time spoke in nearly every debate. It was very
uphill work for some time. The three Villiers and Romilly
stuck to us for some time longer, but the patience of all
the founders of the Society was at last exhausted, except
me and Roebuck. In the season following, 1826-27, things

began to mend. We had acquired two excellent Tory speakers, Hayward and Shee (afterwards Sergeant Shee): the Radical side was reinforced by Charles Buller, Cockburn, and others of the second generation of Cambridge Benthamites; and with their other occasional aid, and the two Tories as well as Roebuck and me for regular speakers, almost every debate was a *bataille rangée* between the "Philosophic Radicals" and the Tory lawyers; until our conflicts were talked about, and several persons of note and consideration came to hear us. This happened still more in the subsequent seasons, 1828 and 1829, when the Coleridgians, in the persons of Maurice and Sterling, made their appearance in the Society as a second Liberal and even Radical party, on totally different grounds from Benthamism and vehemently opposed to it; bringing into these discussions the general doctrines and modes of thought of the European reaction against the philosophy of the eighteenth century; and adding a third and very important belligerent party to our contests, which were now no bad exponent of the movement of opinion among the most cultivated part of the new generation. Our debates were very different from those of common debating societies, for they habitually consisted of the strongest arguments and most philosophic principles which either side was able to produce, thrown often into close and *serré* confutations of one another. The practice was necessarily very useful to us, and eminently so to me. I never, indeed, acquired real fluency, and had always a bad and ungraceful delivery; but I could make myself listened to: and as I always wrote my speeches when, from the feelings involved, or the nature of the ideas to be developed, expression seemed important, I greatly increased my power of effective writing; acquiring not only an ear for smoothness and rhythm, but a practical sense of *telling* sentences, and an immediate criterion of their telling property, by their effect on a mixed audience.

The Society, and the preparation for it, together with the preparation for the morning conversations which were going on simultaneously, occupied the greater part of my leisure; and made me feel it a relief when, in the spring of 1828, I ceased to write for the *Westminster*. The *Review* had fallen into difficulties. Though the sale of the first number had been very encouraging, the permanent sale had never, I believe, been sufficient to pay the expenses, on the scale on which the *Review* was carried on. Those expenses had been considerably, but not sufficiently, reduced. One of the editors, Southern, had resigned; and several of the writers, including my father and me, who had been paid like other contributors for our earlier articles, had latterly written without payment. Nevertheless, the original funds were nearly or quite exhausted, and if the *Review* was to be continued some new arrangement of its affairs had become indispensable. My father and I had several conferences with Bowring on the subject. We were willing to do our utmost for maintaining the *Review* as an organ of our opinions, but not under Bowring's editorship; while the impossibility of its any longer supporting a paid editor afforded a ground on which, without affront to him, we could propose to dispense with his services. We and some of our friends were prepared to carry on the *Review* as unpaid writers, either finding among ourselves an unpaid editor, or sharing the editorship among us. But while this negotiation was proceeding with Bowring's apparent acquiescence, he was carrying on another in a different quarter (with Colonel Perronet Thompson), of which we received the first intimation in a letter from Bowring as editor, informing us merely that an arrangement had been made, and proposing to us to write for the next number, with promise of payment. We did not dispute Bowring's right to bring about, if he could, an arrangement more favourable to himself than the one we had proposed; but we thought the concealment which he had practised towards us, while seemingly entering into our project, an affront; and even had we not thought so, we were indisposed to expend any more of our time and trouble in attempting to write up the *Review* under his management. Accordingly my father excused himself from writing; though two or three years later, on great pressure, he did write one more political article. As for me, I positively refused. And thus ended my connexion with the original *Westminster*. The last article which I wrote in it had cost me more labour than any previous; but it was a labour of love, being a defence of the early French revolutionists against the Tory misrepresentations of Sir Walter Scott,

in the introduction to his *Life of Napoleon.* The number
of books which I read for this purpose, making notes
and extracts—even the number I had to buy (for in
those days there was no public or subscription library from
which books of reference could be taken home), far exceeded the worth of the immediate object; but I had at that
time a half-formed intention of writing a history of the
French Revolution; and though I never executed it, my
collections afterwards were very useful to Carlyle for a
similar purpose.

CHAPTER V.   1826-1832

A CRISIS IN MY MENTAL HISTORY.
ONE STAGE ONWARD

For some years after this time I wrote
very little, and nothing regularly, for publication; and great
were the advantages which I derived from the intermission.
It was of no common importance to me, at this period, to
be able to digest and mature my thoughts for my own mind
only, without any immediate call for giving them out in
print. Had I gone on writing, it would have much dis-
turbed the important transformation in my opinions and
character, which took place during those years. The origin
of this transformation, or at least the process by which I
was prepared for it, can only be explained by turning some
distance back.

From the winter of 1821, when I first read Bentham,
and especially from the commencement of the *Westminster
Review,* I had what might truly be called an object in life;
to be a reformer of the world. My conception of my own

happiness was entirely identified with this object. The personal sympathies I wished for were those of fellow labourers in this enterprise. I endeavoured to pick up as many flowers as I could by the way; but as a serious and permanent personal satisfaction to rest upon, my whole reliance was placed on this; and I was accustomed to felicitate myself on the certainty of a happy life which I enjoyed, through placing my happiness in something durable and distant, in which some progress might be always making, while it could never be exhausted by complete attainment. This did very well for several years, during which the general improvement going on in the world and the idea of myself as engaged with others in struggling to promote it, seemed enough to fill up an interesting and animated existence. But the time came when I awakened from this as from a dream. It was in the autumn of 1826. I was in a dull state of nerves, such as everybody is occasionally liable to; unsusceptible to enjoyment or pleasurable excitement; one of those moods when what is pleasure at other times becomes insipid or indifferent; the state, I should think, in which converts to Methodism usually are, when smitten by their first "conviction of sin." In this frame of mind it occurred to me to put the question directly to myself: "Suppose that all your objects in life were realized; that all the changes in institutions and opinions which you are looking forward to, could be completely effected at this very instant: would this be a great joy and happiness to you?" And an irrepressible self-consciousness distinctly answered, "No!" At this my heart sank within me: the whole foundation on which my life was constructed fell down. All my happiness was to have been found in the continual pursuit of this end. The end had ceased to charm, and how could there ever again be any interest in the means? I seemed to have nothing left to live for.

At first I hoped that the cloud would pass away of itself; but it did not. A night's sleep, the sovereign remedy for the smaller vexations of life, had no effect on it. I awoke to a renewed consciousness of the woeful fact. I carried it with me into all companies, into all occupations. Hardly anything had power to cause me even a few minutes' oblivion of it. For some months the cloud seemed to grow thicker and thicker. The lines in Coleridge's "Dejection"

—I was not then acquainted with them—exactly describe my case:

> A grief without a pang, void, dark and drear,
> A drowsy, stifled, unimpassioned grief,
> Which finds no natural outlet or relief
> In word, or sigh, or tear.

In vain I sought relief from my favourite books; those memorials of past nobleness and greatness from which I had always hitherto drawn strength and animation. I read them now without feeling, or with the accustomed feeling *minus* all its charm; and I became persuaded that my love of mankind, and of excellence for its own sake, had worn itself out. I sought no comfort by speaking to others of what I felt. If I had loved any one sufficiently to make confiding my griefs a necessity, I should not have been in the condition I was. I felt, too, that mine was not an interesting, or in any way respectable distress. There was nothing in it to attract sympathy. Advice, if I had known where to seek it, would have been most precious. The words of Macbeth to the physician often occurred to my thoughts. But there was no one on whom I could build the faintest hope of such assistance. My father, to whom it would have been natural to me to have recourse in any practical difficulties, was the last person to whom, in such a case as this, I looked for help. Everything convinced me that he had no knowledge of any such mental state as I was suffering from, and that even if he could be made to understand it, he was not the physician who could heal it. My education, which was wholly his work, had been conducted without any regard to the possibility of its ending in this result; and I saw no use in giving him the pain of thinking that his plans had failed, when the failure was probably irremediable, and, at all events, beyond the power of *his* remedies. Of other friends I had at that time none to whom I had any hope of making my condition intelligible. It was however abundantly intelligible to myself; and the more I dwelt upon it, the more hopeless it appeared.

My course of study had led me to believe that all mental and moral feelings and qualities, whether of a good or of a bad kind, were the results of association; that we love one thing, and hate another, take pleasure in one sort of action or contemplation, and pain in another sort, through the clinging of pleasurable or painful ideas to those things, from the effect of education or of experience. As a corollary from this, I had always heard it maintained by my father, and was myself convinced, that the object of education should be to form the strongest possible associations of the salutary class; associations of pleasure with all things beneficial to the great whole, and of pain with all things hurtful to it. This doctrine appeared inexpugnable; but it now seemed to me, on retrospect, that my teachers had occupied themselves but superficially with the means of forming and keeping up these salutary associations. They seemed to have trusted altogether to the old familiar instruments, praise and blame, reward and punishment. Now, I did not doubt that by these means, begun early, and applied unremittingly, intense associations of pain and pleasure, especially of pain, might be created, and might produce desires and aversions capable of lasting undiminished to the end of life. But there must always be something artificial and casual in associations thus produced. The pains and pleasures thus forcibly associated with things are not connected with them by any natural tie; and it is therefore, I thought, essential to the durability of these associations, that they should have become so intense and inveterate as to be practically indissoluble before the habitual exercise of the power of analysis had commenced. For I now saw, or thought I saw, what I had always before received with incredulity—that the habit of analysis has a tendency to wear away the feelings; as indeed it has, when no other mental habit is cultivated, and the analysing spirit remains without its natural complements and correctives. The very excellence of analysis (I argued) is that it tends to weaken and undermine whatever is the result of prejudice; that it enables us mentally to separate ideas which have only casually clung together; and no associations whatever could ultimately resist this dissolving force, were it not that we owe to analysis our clearest knowledge of the permanent sequences in nature; the real connexions between things, not dependent on our will and feelings; natural laws, by virtue of which, in many cases, one thing is inseparable from another in fact; which laws, in proportion as they are clearly perceived and imaginatively realized, cause our ideas of things which are always joined together in Nature to cohere more and more closely in our thoughts. Analytic habits may thus even strengthen the associations between causes and effects, means and ends, but tend altogether to weaken those which are, to speak familiarly, a *mere* matter of feeling. They are therefore (I thought) favourable to prudence and clear-sightedness, but a perpetual worm at the root both of the passions and of the virtues; and, above all, fearfully undermine all desires, and all pleasures, which are the effects of association, that is, according to the theory I held, all except the purely physical and organic; of the entire insufficiency of which to make life desirable no one had a stronger conviction than I had. These were the laws of human nature, by which, as it seemed to me, I had been brought to my present state. All those to whom I looked up were of opinion that the pleasure of sympathy with human beings, and the feelings which made the good of others, and especially of mankind on a large scale, the object of existence, were the greatest and surest sources of happiness. Of the truth of this I was convinced, but to know that a feeling would make me happy if I had it, did not give me the feeling. My education, I thought, had failed to create these feelings in sufficient strength to resist the dissolving influences of analysis, while the whole course of my intellectual cultivation had made precocious and premature analysis the inveterate habit of my mind. I was thus, as I said to myself, left stranded at the commencement of my voyage, with a well-equipped ship and a rudder, but no sail; without any real desire for the ends which I had been so carefully fitted out to work for: no delight in virtue, or the general good, but also just as little in anything else. The fountains of vanity and ambition seemed to have dried up within me, as completely as those of benevolence. I had had (as I reflected) some gratification of vanity at too early an age: I had obtained some distinction, and felt myself of some importance, before the desire of distinction and of importance had grown into a passion; and little as it was which I had attained, yet having been attained too early, like all pleasures enjoyed too soon, it had made me blasé and indifferent to the pursuit. Thus neither selfish nor unselfish pleasures were pleasures to me. And there seemed no power in nature sufficient to begin the formation of my character anew, and create, in a mind now irretrievably analytic, fresh associations of pleasure with any of the objects of human desire.

These were the thoughts which mingled with the dry heavy dejection of the melancholy winter of 1826-1827. During this time I was not incapable of my usual occupations. I went on with them mechanically, by the mere force of habit. I had been so drilled in a certain sort of mental exercise that I could still carry it on when all the spirit had gone out of it. I even composed and spoke several speeches at the debating society, how, or with what degree of success, I know not. Of four years continual speaking at that society, this is the only year of which I remember next to nothing. Two lines of Coleridge, in whom alone of all writers I have found a true description of what I felt, were often in my thoughts, not at this time (for I had never read them), but in a later period of the same mental malady:

> Work without hope draws nectar in a sieve,
> And hope without an object cannot live.

In all probability my case was by no means so peculiar as I fancied it, and I doubt not that many others have passed through a similar state; but the idiosyncrasies of my education had given to the general phenomenon a special character, which made it seem the natural effect of causes that it was hardly possible for time to remove. I frequently asked myself, if I could, or if I was bound to go on living, when life must be passed in this manner. I generally answered to myself that I did not think I could possibly bear it beyond a year. When, however, not more than half that duration of time had elapsed, a small ray of light broke in upon my gloom. I was reading, accidentally, Marmontel's *Memoires,* and came to the passage which relates his father's death, the distressed position of the family, and the sudden inspiration by which he, then a mere boy, felt and made them feel that he would be everything to them—would supply the place of all that they had lost. A vivid conception of the scene and its feelings came over me, and I was moved to tears. From this moment my burden grew lighter. The oppression of the thought that all feeling was dead within me was gone. I was no longer hopeless: I was not a stock or a stone. I had still, it seemed, some of the material out of which all worth of character, and all capacity for happiness, are made. Relieved from my ever-present sense of irremediable wretchedness, I gradually found that the ordinary incidents of life could again give me some pleasure; that I could again find enjoyment, not intense, but sufficient for cheerfulness, in sunshine and sky, in books, in conversation, in public affairs; and that there was, once more, excitement, though of a moderate kind, in exerting myself for my opinions, and for the public good. Thus the cloud gradually drew off, and I again enjoyed life; and though I had several relapses, some of which lasted many months, I never again was as miserable as I had been.

The experiences of this period had two very marked effects on my opinions and character. In the first place, they led me to adopt a theory of life, very unlike that on which I had before acted, and having much in common with what at that time I certainly had never heard of, the anti-self-consciousness theory of Carlyle. I never, indeed, wavered in the conviction that happiness is the test of all rules of conduct, and the end of life. But I now thought that this end was only to be attained by not making it the direct end. Those only are happy (I thought) who have their minds fixed on some object other than their own happiness; on the happiness of others, on the improvement of mankind, even on some art or pursuit, followed not as a means, but as itself an ideal end. Aiming thus at something else, they find happiness by the way. The enjoyments of life (such was now my theory) are sufficient to make it a pleasant thing, when they are taken *en passant,* without being made a principal object. Once make them so, and they are immediately felt to be insufficient. They will not bear a scrutinizing examination. Ask yourself whether you are happy, and you cease to be so. The only chance is to treat, not happiness, but some end external to it, as the purpose of life. Let your self-consciousness, your scrutiny, your self-interrogation, exhaust themselves on that; and if otherwise fortunately circumstanced, you will inhale happiness with the air you breathe, without dwelling on it or thinking about it, without either forestalling it in imagination, or putting it

to flight by fatal questioning. This theory now became
the basis of my philosophy of life. And I still hold to it
as the best theory for all those who have but a moderate
degree of sensibility and of capacity for enjoyment, that
is, for the great majority of mankind.

The other important change which my opinions at this
time underwent was that I, for the first time, gave its
proper place, among the prime necessities of human well-
being, to the internal culture of the individual. I ceased
to attach almost exclusive importance to the ordering
of outward circumstances, and the training of the human
being for speculation and for action.

I had now learnt by experience that the passive susceptibilities needed to be cultivated as well as the active
capacities, and required to be nourished and enriched as
well as guided. I did not, for an instant, lose sight of, or
undervalue, that part of the truth which I had seen before;
I never turned recreant to intellectual culture, or ceased
to consider the power and practice of analysis as an essential condition both of individual and of social improvement. But I thought that it had consequences which
required to be corrected, by joining other kinds of cultivation with it. The maintenance of a due balance among the
faculties now seemed to me of primary importance. The
cultivation of the feelings became one of the cardinal
points in my ethical and philosophical creed. And my
thoughts and inclinations turned in an increasing degree
towards whatever seemed capable of being instrumental
to that object.

I now began to find meaning in the things which I
had read or heard about the importance of poetry and
art as instruments of human culture. But it was some
time longer before I began to know this by personal experience. The only one of the imaginative arts in which
I had from childhood taken great pleasure was music;
the best effect of which (and in this it surpasses perhaps
every other art) consists in exciting enthusiasm; in wind-
ing up to a high pitch those feelings of an elevated kind
which are already in the character, but to which this
excitement gives a glow and a fervour, which, though
transitory at its utmost height, is precious for sustain-
ing them at other times. This effect of music I had often
experienced; but like all my pleasurable susceptibilities

it was suspended during the gloomy period. I had sought
relief again and again from this quarter, but found none.
After the tide had turned, and I was in process of recovery, I had been helped forward by music, but in a
much less elevated manner. I at this time first became acquainted with Weber's *Oberon,* and the extreme pleasure
which I drew from its delicious melodies did me good, by
showing me a source of pleasure to which I was as susceptible as ever. The good, however, was much impaired
by the thought that the pleasure of music (as is quite
true of such pleasure as this was, that of mere tune) fades
with familiarity, and requires either to be revived by in-
termittence, or fed by continual novelty. And it is very
characteristic both of my then state, and of the general
tone of my mind at this period of my life, that I was
seriously tormented by the thought of the exhaustibility of
musical combinations. The octave consists only of five
tones and two semitones, which can be put together in
only a limited number of ways, of which but a small proportion are beautiful; most of these, it seemed to me, must
have been already discovered, and there could not be room
for a long succession of Mozarts and Webers to strike
out, as these had done, entirely new and surpassingly
rich veins of musical beauty. This source of anxiety may,
perhaps, be thought to resemble that of the philosophers
of Laputa, who feared lest the sun should be burnt out.
It was, however, connected with the best feature in my
character, and the only good point to be found in my
very unromantic and in no way honourable distress. For
though my dejection, honestly looked at, could not be
called other than egotistical, produced by the ruin, as I
thought, of my fabric of happiness, yet the destiny of mankind in general was ever in my thoughts, and could not
be separated from my own. I felt that the flaw in my life
must be a flaw in life itself; that the question was, whether,
if the reformers of society and government could succeed
in their objects, and every person in the community were
free and in a state of physical comfort, the pleasures
of life, being no longer kept up by struggle and privation,
would cease to be pleasures. And I felt that unless I could
see my way to some better hope than this for human happiness in general, my dejection must continue; but that if I
could see such an outlet, I should then look on the world

with pleasure; content, as far as I was myself concerned, with any fair share of the general lot.

This state of my thoughts and feelings made the fact of my reading Wordsworth for the first time (in the autumn of 1828), an important event in my life. I took up the collection of his poems from curiosity, with no expectation of mental relief from it, though I had before resorted to poetry with that hope. In the worst period of my depression, I had read through the whole of Byron (then new to me), to try whether a poet, whose peculiar department was supposed to be that of the intenser feelings, could rouse any feeling in me. As might be expected, I got no good from this reading, but the reverse. The poet's state of mind was too like my own. His was the lament of a man who had worn out all pleasures, and who seemed to think that life, to all who possess the good things of it, must necessarily be the vapid, uninteresting thing which I found it. His *Harold* and *Manfred* had the same burden on them which I had; and I was not in a frame of mind to desire any comfort from the vehement sensual passion of his Giaours, or the sullenness of his Laras. But while Byron was exactly what did not suit my condition, Wordsworth was exactly what did. I had looked into the *Excursion* two or three years before, and found little in it; and I should probably have found as little, had I read it at this time. But the miscellaneous poems, in the two-volume edition of 1815 (to which little of value was added in the latter part of the author's life), proved to be the precise thing for my mental wants at that particular juncture.

In the first place, these poems addressed themselves powerfully to one of the strongest of my pleasurable susceptibilities, the love of rural objects and natural scenery; to which I had been indebted not only for much of the pleasure of my life, but quite recently for relief from one of my longest relapses into depression. In this power of rural beauty over me, there was a foundation laid for taking pleasure in Wordsworth's poetry; the more so as his scenery lies mostly among mountains, which, owing to my early Pyrenean excursion, were my ideal of natural beauty. But Wordsworth would never have had any great effect on me if he had merely placed before me beautiful pictures of natural scenery. Scott does this

still better than Wordsworth, and a very second-rate
landscape does it more effectually than any poet. What
made Wordsworth's poems a medicine for my state of
mind was that they expressed not mere outward beauty,
but states of feeling, and of thought coloured by feeling,
under the excitement of beauty. They seemed to be the
very culture of the feelings, which I was in quest of. In
them I seemed to draw from a source of inward joy, of
sympathetic and imaginative pleasure, which could be
shared in by all human beings; which had no connexion
with struggle or imperfection, but would be made richer
by every improvement in the physical or social condition
of mankind. From them I seemed to learn what would
be the perennial sources of happiness when all the greater
evils of life shall have been removed. And I felt myself
at once better and happier as I came under their influence.
There have certainly been, even in our own age, greater
poets than Wordsworth; but poetry of deeper and loftier
feeling could not have done for me at that time what his
did. I needed to be made to feel that there was real, permanent happiness in tranquil contemplation. Wordsworth
taught me this, not only without turning away from, but
with a greatly increased interest in the common feelings
and common destiny of human beings. And the delight
which these poems gave me proved that with culture of
this sort there was nothing to dread from the most confirmed habit of analysis. At the conclusion of the *Poems*
came the famous ode, falsely called Platonic, "Intimations
of Immortality"; in which, along with more than his
usual sweetness of melody and rhythm, and along with the
two passages of grand imagery but bad philosophy so
often quoted, I found that he too had had similar experience to mine; that he also had felt that the first freshness of youthful enjoyment of life was not lasting; but that
he had sought for compensation, and found it, in the way
in which he was now teaching me to find it. The result
was that I gradually, but completely, emerged from my
habitual depression, and was never again subject to it.
I long continued to value Wordsworth less according to
his intrinsic merits than by the measure of what he had
done for me. Compared with the greatest poets, he may be
said to be the poet of unpoetical natures, possessed of
quiet and contemplative tastes. But unpoetical natures are

precisely those which require poetic cultivation. This cultivation Wordsworth is much more fitted to give than poets who are intrinsically far more poets than he.

It so fell out that the merits of Wordsworth were the occasion of my first public declaration of my new way of thinking, and separation from those of my habitual companions who had not undergone a similar change. The person with whom at that time I was most in the habit of comparing notes on such subjects was Roebuck, and I induced him to read Wordsworth, in whom he also at first seemed to find much to admire; but I, like most Wordsworthians, threw myself into strong antagonism to Byron, both as a poet and as to his influence on the character. Roebuck, all whose instincts were those of action and struggle, had, on the contrary, a strong relish and great admiration of Byron, whose writings he regarded as the poetry of human life, while Wordsworth's, according to him, was that of flowers and butterflies. We agreed to have the fight out at our Debating Society, where we accordingly discussed for two evenings the comparative merits of Byron and Wordsworth, propounding and illustrating by long recitations our respective theories of poetry; Sterling also, in a brilliant speech, putting forward his particular theory. This was the first debate on any weighty subject in which Roebuck and I had been on opposite sides. The schism between us widened from this time more and more, though we continued for some years longer to be companions. In the beginning, our chief divergence related to the cultivation of the feelings. Roebuck was in many respects very different from the vulgar notion of a Benthamite or Utilitarian. He was a lover of poetry and of most of the fine arts. He took great pleasure in music, in dramatic performances, especially in painting, and himself drew and designed landscapes with great facility and beauty. But he never could be made to see that these things have any value as aids in the formation of character. Personally, instead of being, as Benthamites are supposed to be, void of feeling, he had very quick and strong sensibilities. But, like most Englishmen who have feelings, he found his feelings stand very much in his way. He was much more susceptible to the painful sympathies than to the pleasurable, and looking for his happiness elsewhere, he wished that his feelings should be

deadened rather than quickened. And, in truth, the English character, and English social circumstances, make it
so seldom possible to derive happiness from the exercise
of the sympathies that it is not wonderful if they count for
little in an Englishman's scheme of life. In most other
countries the paramount importance of the sympathies
as a constituent of individual happiness is an axiom, taken
for granted rather than needing any formal statement;
but most English thinkers seem to regard them as necessary evils, required for keeping men's actions benevolent
and compassionate. Roebuck was, or appeared to be, this
kind of Englishman. He saw little good in any cultivation
of the feelings, and none at all in cultivating them through
the imagination, which he thought was only cultivating
illusions. It was in vain I urged on him that the imaginative
emotion which an idea, when vividly conceived, excites
in us, is not an illusion but a fact, as real as any of the
other qualities of objects; and, far from implying anything
erroneous and delusive in our mental apprehension of the
object, is quite consistent with the most accurate knowledge and most perfect practical recognition of all its
physical and intellectual laws and relations. The intensest
feeling of the beauty of a cloud lighted by the setting sun
is no hindrance to my knowing that the cloud is a vapour
of water, subject to all the laws of vapours in a state of
suspension; and I am just as likely to allow for, and
act on, these physical laws whenever there is occasion to
do so, as if I had been incapable of perceiving any
distinction between beauty and ugliness.

While my intimacy with Roebuck diminished, I fell
more and more into friendly intercourse with our Coleridgian adversaries in the Society, Frederick Maurice and
John Sterling, both subsequently so well known, the former
by his writings, the latter through the biographies by Hare
and Carlyle. Of these two friends, Maurice was the
thinker, Sterling the orator, and impassioned expositor
of thoughts which, at this period, were almost entirely
formed for him by Maurice.

With Maurice I had for some time been acquainted
through Eyton Tooke, who had known him at Cambridge,
and although my discussions with him were almost always
disputes, I had carried away from them much that helped
to build up my new fabric of thought, in the same way

as I was deriving much from Coleridge, and from the writings of Goethe and other German authors which I read during these years. I have so deep a respect for Maurice's character and purposes, as well as for his great mental gifts, that it is with some unwillingness I say anything which may seem to place him on a less high eminence than I would gladly be able to accord him. But I have always thought that there was more intellectual power wasted in Maurice than in any other of my contemporaries. Few of them certainly have had so much to waste. Great powers of generalization, rare ingenuity and subtlety, and a wide perception of important and unobvious truths, served him not for putting something better into the place of the worthless heap of received opinions on the great subjects of thought, but for proving to his own mind that the Church of England had known everything from the first, and that all the truths on the ground of which the Church and orthodoxy have been attacked (many of which he saw as clearly as any one) are not only consistent with the Thirty-nine Articles, but are better understood and expressed in those Articles than by any one who rejects them. I have never been able to find any other explanation of this than by attributing it to that timidity of conscience, combined with original sensitiveness of temperament, which has so often driven highly gifted men into Romanism from the need of a firmer support than they can find in the independent conclusions of their own judgment. Any more vulgar kind of timidity no one who knew Maurice would ever think of imputing to him, even if he had not given public proof of his freedom from it by his ultimate collision with some of the opinions commonly regarded as orthodox, and by his noble origination of the Christian Socialist movement. The nearest parallel to him, in a moral point of view, is Coleridge, to whom, in merely intellectual power, apart from poetical genius, I think him decidedly superior. At this time, however, he might be described as a disciple of Coleridge, and Sterling as a disciple of Coleridge and of him. The modifications which were taking place in my old opinions gave me some points of contact with them; and both Maurice and Sterling were of considerable use to my development. With Sterling I soon became very intimate, and was more attached to him than I have ever been to any other man.

He was indeed one of the most lovable of men. His frank, cordial, affectionate, and expansive character; a love of truth alike conspicuous in the highest things and the humblest; a generous and ardent nature which threw itself with impetuosity into the opinions it adopted, but was as eager to do justice to the doctrines and the men it was opposed to as to make war on what it thought their errors; and an equal devotion to the two cardinal points of liberty and duty formed a combination of qualities as attractive to me as to all others who knew him as well as I did. With his open mind and heart, he found no difficulty in joining hands with me across the gulf which as yet divided our opinions. He told me how he and others had looked upon me (from hearsay information), as a "made" or manufactured man, having had a certain impress of opinion stamped on me which I could only reproduce; and what a change took place in his feelings when he found, in the discussion on Wordsworth and Byron, that Wordsworth, and all which that name implies, "belonged" to me as much as to him and his friends. The failure of his health soon scattered all his plans of life, and compelled him to live at a distance from London, so that after the first year or two of our acquaintance, we only saw each other at distant intervals. But (as he said himself in one of his letters to Carlyle), when we did meet it was like brothers. Though he was never, in the full sense of the word, a profound thinker, his openness of mind, and the moral courage in which he greatly surpassed Maurice, made him outgrow the dominion which Maurice and Coleridge had once exercised over his intellect; though he retained to the last a great but discriminating admiration of both, and towards Maurice a warm affection. Except in that short and transistory phasis of his life, during which he made the mistake of becoming a clergyman, his mind was ever progressive; and the advance he always seemed to have made when I saw him after an interval, made me apply to him what Goethe said of Schiller, "er hatte ein fürchterliche Fortschreitung." He and I started from intellectual points almost as wide apart as the poles, but the distance between us was always diminishing: if I made steps towards some of his opinions, he, during his short life, was constantly approximating more and more to several of mine; and if he had lived, and had health and vigour to prosecute his ever-assiduous self-culture, there is no knowing how much further this spontaneous assimilation might have proceeded.

After 1829 I withdrew from attendance on the Debating Society. I had had enough of speech-making, and was glad to carry on my private studies and meditations without any immediate call for outward assertion of their results. I found the fabric of my old and taught opinions giving way in many fresh places, and I never allowed it to fall to pieces, but was incessantly occupied in weaving it anew. I never, in the course of my transition, was content to remain, for ever so short a time, confused and unsettled. When I had taken in any new idea, I could not rest till I had adjusted its relation to my old opinions, and ascertained exactly how far its effect ought to extend in modifying or superseding them.

The conflicts which I had so often had to sustain in defending the theory of government laid down in Bentham's and my father's writings, and the acquaintance I had obtained with other schools of political thinking, made me aware of many things which that doctrine, professing to be a theory of government in general, ought to have made room for, and did not. But these things, as yet, remained with me rather as corrections to be made in applying the theory to practice, than as defects in the theory. I felt that politics could not be a science of specific experience; and that the accusations against the Benthamic theory of being a theory, of proceeding a priori by way of general reasoning, instead of Baconian experiment, showed complete ignorance of Bacon's principles, and of the necessary conditions of experimental investigation. At this juncture appeared in the *Edinburgh Review*, Macaulay's famous attack on my father's *Essay on Government*. This gave me much to think about. I saw that Macaulay's conception of the logic of politics was erroneous; that he stood up for the empirical mode of treating political phenomena, against the philosophical; that even in physical science his notions of philosophizing might have recognized Kepler, but would have excluded Newton and Laplace. But I could not help feeling that though the tone was unbecoming (an error for which the writer, at a later period, made the most ample and honourable amends), there was truth in several of his

strictures on my father's treatment of the subject; that
my father's premises were really too narrow, and included but a small number of the general truths on
which, in politics, the important consequences depend.
Identity of interest between the governing body and the
community at large is not, in any practical sense which
can be attached to it, the only thing on which good government depends; neither can this identity of interest be secured by the mere conditions of election. I was not at all
satisfied with the mode in which my father met the criticisms of Macaulay. He did not, as I thought he ought to
have done, justify himself by saying, "I was not writing a
scientific treatise on politics, I was writing an argument for
parliamentary reform." He treated Macaulay's argument
as simply irrational; an attack upon the reasoning faculty;
an example of the saying of Hobbes that when reason is
against a man, a man will be against reason. This made me
think that there was really something more fundamentally
erroneous in my father's conception of philosophical
method, as applicable to politics, than I had hitherto supposed there was. But I did not at first see clearly what
the error might be. At last it flashed upon me all at once
in the course of other studies. In the early part of 1830
I had begun to put on paper the ideas on logic (chiefly
on the distinctions among terms, and the import of propositions) which had been suggested and in part worked
out in the morning conversations already spoken of. Having secured these thoughts from being lost, I pushed on
into the other parts of the subject to try whether I could
do anything further towards clearing up the theory of
logic generally. I grappled at once with the problem of
induction, postponing that of reasoning, on the ground that
it is necessary to obtain premises before we can reason
from them. Now, induction is mainly a process for finding the causes of effects; and in attempting to fathom
the mode of tracing causes and effects in physical science,
I soon saw that in the more perfect of the sciences,
we ascend, by generalization from particulars to the tendencies of causes considered singly, and then reason down-
ward from those separate tendencies to the effect of the
same causes when combined. I then asked myself, what is
the ultimate analysis of this deductive process; the common theory of the syllogism evidently throwing no light

upon it. My practice (learnt from Hobbes and my father) being to study abstract principles by means of the best concrete instances I could find, the Composition of Forces, in dynamics, occurred to me as the most complete example of the logical process I was investigating. On examining, accordingly, what the mind does when it applies the principle of the Composition of Forces, I found that it performs a simple act of addition. It adds the separate effect of the one force to the separate effect of the other, and puts down the sum of these separate effects as the joint effect. But is this a legitimate process? In dynamics, and in all the mathematical branches of physics, it is; but in some other cases, as in chemistry, it is not; and I then recollected that something not unlike this was pointed out as one of the distinctions between chemical and mechanical phenomena in the introduction to that favourite of my boyhood, Thompson's *System of Chemistry*. This distinction at once made my mind clear as to what was perplexing me in respect to the philosophy of politics. I now saw that a science is either deductive or experimental, according as, in the province it deals with, the effects of causes when conjoined are or are not the sums of the effects which the same causes produce when separate. It followed that politics must be a deductive science. It thus appeared that both Macaulay and my father were wrong; the one in assimilating the method of philosophizing in politics to the purely experimental method of chemistry; while the other, though right in adopting a deductive method, had made a wrong selection of one, having taken as the type of deduction branches of natural philosophy, but the inappropriate one of pure geometry, which, not being a science of causation of all, does not require or admit of any summing-up of effects. A foundation was thus laid in my thoughts for the principal chapters of what I afterwards published on the "Logic of the Moral Sciences"; and my new position in respect to my old political creed now became perfectly definite.

If I am asked, what system of political philosophy I substituted for that which, as a philosophy, I had abandoned, I answer, no system: only a conviction that the true system was something much more complex and many-sided than I had previously had any idea of, and that its office was to supply not a set of model institutions, but principles from which the institutions suitable to any given circumstances might be deduced. The influences of European, that is to say, continental, thought, and especially those of the reaction of the nineteenth century against the eighteenth, were now streaming in upon me. They came from various quarters: from the writings of Coleridge, which I had begun to read with interest even before the change in my opinions; from the Coleridgians with whom I was in personal intercourse; from what I had read of Goethe; from Carlyle's early articles in the *Edinburgh* and *Foreign Reviews,* though for a long time I saw nothing in these (as my father saw nothing in them to the last) but insane rhapsody. From these sources, and from the acquaintance I kept up with the French literature of the time, I derived, among other ideas which the general turning upside down of the opinions of European thinkers had brought uppermost, these in particular: That the human mind has a certain order of possible progress, in which some things must precede others, an order which governments and public instructors can modify to some, but not to an unlimited extent; that all questions of political institutions are relative, not absolute, and that different stages of human progress not only *will* have, but *ought* to have, different institutions; that government is always either in the hands, or passing into the hands, of whatever is the strongest power in society, and that what this power is does not depend on institutions, but institutions on it; that any general theory or philosophy of politics supposes a previous theory of human progress, and that this is the same thing with a philosophy of history. These opinions, true in the main, were held in an exaggerated and violent manner by the thinkers with whom I was now most accustomed to compare notes, and who, as usual with a reaction, ignored that half of the truth which the thinkers of the eighteenth century saw. But though, at one period of my progress, I for some time undervalued that great century, I never joined in the reaction against it, but kept as firm hold of one side of the truth as I took of the other. The fight between the nineteenth century and the eighteenth always reminded me of the battle about the shield, one side of which was white and the other black. I marvelled at the blind rage with which the combatants rushed against one another. I

applied to them, and to Coleridge himself, many of
Coleridge's sayings about half-truths; and Goethe's de-
vice, "many-sidedness," was one which I would most
willingly, at this period, have taken for mine.

The writers by whom, more than by any others, a
new mode of political thinking was brought home to me,
were those of the Saint-Simonian school in France. In
1829 and 1830 I became acquainted with some of their
writings. They were then only in the earlier stages of
their speculations. They had not yet dressed out their
philosophy as a religion, nor had they organized their
scheme of socialism. They were just beginning to question
the principle of hereditary property. I was by no means
prepared to go with them even this length; but I was greatly struck with the connected view, which they for the first
time presented to me, of the natural order of human progress; and especially with their division of all history into
organic periods and critical periods. During the organic
periods (they said) mankind accept with firm conviction
some positive creed, claiming jurisdiction over all their
actions, and containing more or less of truth and adapta-
tion to the needs of humanity. Under its influence they
make all the progress compatible with the creed, and
finally outgrow it; when a period follows of criticism and
negation, in which mankind lose their old convictions
without acquiring any new ones of a general or authoritative character, except the conviction that the old are false.
The period of Greek and Roman polytheism, so long as
really believed in by instructed Greeks and Romans, was
an organic period, succeeded by the critical or sceptical
period of the Greek philosophers. Another organic period
came in with Christianity. The corresponding critical
period began with the Reformation, has lasted ever since,
still lasts, and cannot altogether cease until a new organic
period has been inaugurated by the triumph of a yet more
advanced creed. These ideas, I knew, were not peculiar
to the Saint-Simonians; on the contrary, they were the
general property of Europe, or at least of Germany and
France, but they had never, to my knowledge, been so
completely systematized as by these writers, nor the
distinguishing characteristics of a critical period so powerfully set forth; for I was not then acquainted with Fichte's
lectures on "The Characteristics of the Present Age." In

Carlyle, indeed, I found bitter denunciations of an "age of unbelief," and of the present age as such, which I, like most people at that time, supposed to be passionate protests in favour of the old modes of belief. But all that was true in these denunciations I thought that I found more calmly and philosophically stated by the Saint-Simonians. Among their publications, too, there was one which seemed to me far superior to the rest; in which the general idea was matured into something much more definite and instructive. This was an early work of Auguste Comte, who then called himself, and even announced himself in the title-page as a pupil of Saint-Simon. In this tract M. Comte first put forth the doctrine, which he afterwards so copiously illustrated, of the natural succession of three stages in every department of human knowledge: first, the theological, next the metaphysical, and lastly, the positive stage; and contended, that social science must be subject to the same law; that the feudal and Catholic system was the concluding phasis of the theological state of the social science, Protestantism the commencement, and the doctrines of the French Revolution the consummation, of the metaphysical; and that its positive state was yet to come. This doctrine harmonized well with my existing notions, to which it seemed to give a scientific shape. I already regarded the methods of physical science as the proper models for political. But the chief benefit which I derived at this time from the trains of thought suggested by the Saint-Simonians and by Comte, was that I obtained a clearer conception than ever before of the peculiarities of an era of transition in opinion, and ceased to mistake the moral and intellectual characteristics of such an era for the normal attributes of humanity. I looked forward, through the present age of loud disputes but generally weak convictions, to a future which shall unite the best qualities of the critical with the best qualities of the organic periods; unchecked liberty of thought, unbounded freedom of individual action in all modes not hurtful to others; but also, convictions as to what is right and wrong, useful and pernicious, deeply engraven on the feelings by early education and general unanimity of sentiment, and so firmly grounded in reason and in the true exigencies of life that they shall not, like all former and present creeds, religious, ethical, and political,

require to be periodically thrown off and replaced by
others.

M. Comte soon left the Saint-Simonians, and I lost
sight of him and his writings for a number of years. But
the Saint-Simonians I continued to cultivate. I was kept
au courant of their progress by one of their most enthusiastic disciples, M. Gustave d'Eichthal, who about that
time passed a considerable interval in England. I was
introduced to their chiefs, Bazard and Enfantin, in 1830;
and as long as their public teachings and proselytism
continued I read nearly everything they wrote. Their
criticisms on the common doctrines of liberalism seemed
to me full of important truth; and it was partly by their
writings that my eyes were opened to the very limited
and temporary value of the old political economy, which
assumes private property and inheritance as indefeasible
facts, and freedom of production and exchange as the
dernier mot of social improvement. The scheme gradually
unfolded by the Saint-Simonians, under which the labour
and capital of society would be managed for the general
account of the community, every individual being required
to take a share of labour, either as thinker, teacher, artist,
or producer, all being classed according to their capacity,
and remunerated according to their work, appeared to me
a far superior description of socialism to Owen's. Their
aim seemed to me desirable and rational, however their
means might be inefficacious; and though I neither believed in the practicability, nor in the beneficial operation
of their social machinery, I felt that the proclamation of
such an ideal of human society could not but tend to give
a beneficial direction to the efforts of others to bring
society, as at present constituted, nearer to some ideal
standard. I honoured them most of all for what they have
been most cried down for—the boldness and freedom
from prejudice with which they treated the subject of
family, the most important of any, and needing more
fundamental alterations than remain to be made in any
other great social institution, but on which scarcely any
reformer has the courage to touch. In proclaiming the
perfect equality of men and women, and an entirely new
order of things in regard to their relations with one another, the Saint-Simonians, in common with Owen and

Fourier, have entitled themselves to the grateful remembrance of future generations.

In giving an account of this period of my life, I have
only specified such of my new impressions as appeared
to me, both at the time and since, to be a kind of turning points, marking a definite progress in my mode of
thought. But these few selected points give a very insufficient idea of the quantity of thinking which I carried
on respecting a host of subjects during these years of
transition. Much of this, it is true, consisted in rediscover-
ing things known to all the world, which I had previously
disbelieved, or disregarded. But the rediscovery was to me
a discovery, giving me plenary possession of the truths,
not as traditional platitudes, but fresh from their source;
and it seldom failed to place them in some new light, by
which they were reconciled with, and seemed to confirm,
while they modified, the truths less generally known which
lay in my early opinions, and in no essential part of which
I at any time wavered. All my new thinking only laid the
foundation of these more deeply and strongly, while it
often removed misapprehension and confusion of ideas
which had perverted their effect. For example, during the
later returns of my dejection, the doctrine of what is
called philosophical necessity weighed on my existence
like an incubus. I felt as if I was scientifically proved to
be the helpless slave of antecedent circumstances; as if
my character and that of all others had been formed for
us by agencies beyond our control, and was wholly out
of our own power. I often said to myself, what a relief
it would be if I could disbelieve the doctrine of the formation of character by circumstances; and remembering the
wish of Fox respecting the doctrine of resistance to governments, that it might never be forgotten by kings, nor
remembered by subjects, I said that it would be a blessing
if the doctrine of necessity could be believed by all *quoad*
the characters of others, and disbelieved in regard to their
own. I pondered painfully on the subject, till gradually I
saw light through it. I perceived that the word necessity, as
a name for the doctrine of cause and effect applied to
human action, carried with it a misleading association;
and that this association was the operative force in the
depressing and paralysing influence which I had experienced: I saw that though our character is formed by cir-

cumstances, our own desires can do much to shape those circumstances; and that what is really inspiring and ennobling in the doctrine of free will is the conviction that we have real power over the formation of our own character; that our will, by influencing some of our circumstances, can modify our future habits or capabilities of willing. All this was entirely consistent with the doctrine of circumstances, or rather, was that doctrine itself, properly understood. From that time I drew in my own mind a clear distinction between the doctrine of circumstances, and fatalism; discarding altogether the misleading word necessity. The theory, which I now for the first time rightly apprehended, ceased altogether to be discouraging, and besides the relief to my spirits, I no longer suffered under the burden, so heavy to one who aims at being a reformer in opinions, of thinking one doctrine true, and the contrary doctrine morally beneficial. The train of thought which had extricated me from this dilemma seemed to me, in after years, fitted to render a similar service to others; and it now forms the chapter on "Liberty and Necessity" in the concluding book of my *System of Logic*.

Again, in politics, though I no longer accepted the doctrine of the *Essay on Government* as a scientific theory; though I ceased to consider representative democracy as an absolute principle, and regarded it as a question of time, place, and circumstance; though I now looked upon the choice of political institutions as a moral and educational question more than one of material interests, thinking that it ought to be decided mainly by the consideration, what great improvement in life and culture stands next in order for the people concerned as the condition of their further progress, and what institutions are most likely to promote that; nevertheless, this change in the premises of my political philosophy did not alter my practical political creed as to the requirements of my own time and country. I was as much as ever a Radical and Democrat for Europe, and especially for England. I thought the predominance of the aristocratic classes, the noble and the rich, in the English constitution, an evil worth any struggle to get rid of; not on account of taxes, or any such comparatively small inconvenience, but as the great demoralizing agency in the country. Demoralizing, first, because it made the conduct of the Government an example of gross public

immorality, through the predominance of private over
public interests in the State, and the abuse of the powers
of legislation for the advantage of classes. Secondly, and
in a still greater degree, because the respect of the multitude always attaching itself principally to that which, in
the existing state of society, is the chief passport to power;
and under English institutions, riches, hereditary or acquired, being the almost exclusive source of political importance; riches, and the signs of riches, were almost the
only things really respected, and the life of the people was
mainly devoted to the pursuit of them. I thought that
while the higher and richer classes held the power of
government, the instruction and improvement of the mass
of the people were contrary to the self-interest of those
classes, because tending to render the people more powerful for throwing off the yoke; but if the democracy obtained a large, and perhaps the principal share, in the
governing power, it would become the interest of the
opulent classes to promote their education, in order to
ward off really mischievous errors, and especially those
which would lead to unjust violations of property. On
these grounds I was not only as ardent as ever for democratic institutions, but earnestly hoped that Owenite, Saint-
Simonian, and all other anti-property doctrines might
spread widely among the poorer classes; not that I thought
those doctrines true, or desired that they should be acted
on, but in order that the higher classes might be made
to see that they had more to fear from the poor when
uneducated, than when educated.

In this frame of mind the French Revolution of July
found me. It roused my utmost enthusiasm, and gave me,
as it were, a new existence. I went at once to Paris, was
introduced to Lafayette, and laid the groundwork of the
intercourse I afterwards kept up with several of the active
chiefs of the extreme popular party. After my return I entered warmly, as a writer, into the political discussions of
the time; which soon became still more exciting, by the
coming in of Lord Grey's Ministry, and the proposing of
the Reform Bill. For the next few years I wrote copiously
in newspapers. It was about this time that Fonblanque,
who had for some time written the political articles in the
Examiner, became the proprietor and editor of the paper.
It is not forgotten with what verve and talent, as well as

fine wit, he carried it on, during the whole period of Lord Grey's Ministry, and what importance it assumed as the principal representative, in the newspaper press, of Radical opinions. The distinguishing character of the paper was given to it entirely by his own articles, which formed at least three-fourths of all the original writing contained in it; but of the remaining fourth I contributed during those years a much larger share than anyone else. I wrote nearly all the articles on French subjects, including a weekly summary of French politics, often extending to considerable length; together with many leading articles on general politics, commercial and financial legislation, and any miscellaneous subjects in which I felt interested, and which were suitable to the paper, including occasional reviews of books. Mere newspaper articles on the occurrences or questions of the moment gave no opportunity for the development of any general mode of thought; but I attempted in the beginning of 1831, to embody in a series of articles, headed "The Spirit of the Age," some of my new opinions, and especially to point out in the character of the present age, the anomalies and evils characteristic of the transition from a system of opinions which had worn out, to another only in process of being formed. These articles were, I fancy, lumbering in style, and not lively or striking enough to be at any time, acceptable to newspaper readers; but had they been far more attractive, still, at that particular moment, when great political changes were impending and engrossing all minds, these discussions were ill timed, and missed fire altogether. The only effect which I know to have been produced by them was that Carlyle, then living in a secluded part of Scotland, read them in his solitude, and saying to himself (as he afterwards told me) "Here is a new mystic," inquired on coming to London that autumn respecting their authorship; an inquiry which was the immediate cause of our becoming personally acquainted.

I have already mentioned Carlyle's earlier writings as one of the channels through which I received the influences which enlarged my early narrow creed; but I do not think that those writings, by themselves, would ever have had any effect on my opinions. What truths they contained, though of the very kind which I was already receiving from other quarters, were presented in a form and vesture less suited than any other to give them access to a mind trained as mine had been. They seemed a haze of poetry and German metaphysics, in which almost the only clear thing was a strong animosity to most of the opinions which were the basis of my mode of thought: religious scepticism, utilitarianism, the doctrine of circumstances, and the attaching any importance to democracy, logic, or political economy. Instead of my having been taught anything, in the first instance, by Carlyle, it was only in proportion as I came to see the same truths through media more suited to my mental constitution that I recognized them in his writings. Then, indeed, the wonderful power with which he put them forth made a deep impression upon me, and I was during a long period one of his most fervent admirers; but the good his writings did me was not as philosophy to instruct, but as poetry to animate. Even at the time when our acquaintance commenced, I was not sufficiently advanced in my new modes of thought to appreciate him fully; a proof of which is, that on his showing me the manuscript of *Sartor Resartus*, his best and greatest work, which he had just then finished, I made little of it; though when it came out about two years afterwards in *Fraser's Magazine* I read it with enthusiastic admiration and the keenest delight. I did not seek and cultivate Carlyle less on account of the fundamental differences in our philosophy. He soon found out that I was not "another mystic," and when for the sake of my own integrity I wrote to him a distinct profession of all those of my opinions which I knew he most disliked, he replied that the chief difference between us was that I "was as yet consciously nothing of a mystic." I do not know at what period he gave up the expectation that I was destined to become one; but though both his and my opinions underwent in subsequent years considerable changes, we never approached much nearer to each other's modes of thought than we were in the first years of our acquaintance. I did not, however, deem myself a competent judge of Carlyle. I felt that he was a poet, and that I was not; that he was a man of intuition, which I was not; and that as such, he not only saw many things long before me, which I could only when they were pointed out to me, hobble after and prove, but that it was highly probable he could see many things which were not visible

to me even after they were pointed out. I knew that I could
not see round him, and could never be certain that I saw
over him; and I never presumed to judge him with any
definiteness, until he was interpreted to me by one greatly
the superior of us both—who was more a poet than he,
and more a thinker than I—whose own mind and nature
included his, and infinitely more.

Among the persons of intellect whom I had known
of old, the one with whom I had now most points of
agreement was the elder Austin. I have mentioned that he
always set himself in opposition to our early sectarianism;
and latterly he had, like myself, come under new influences. Having been appointed Professor of Jurisprudence in the London University (now University College),
he had lived for some time at Bonn to study for his
lectures; and the influences of German literature and of
the German character and state of society had made a very
perceptible change in his views of life. His personal disposition was much softened; he was less militant and
polemic; his tastes had begun to turn themselves towards
the poetic and contemplative. He attached much less importance than formerly to outward changes; unless accompanied by a better cultivation of the inward nature.
He had a strong distaste for the general meanness of
English life, the absence of enlarged thoughts and unselfish desires, the low objects on which the faculties
of all classes of the English are intent. Even the kind of
public interests which Englishmen care for, he held in
very little esteem. He thought that there was more practical good government, and (which is true enough) infinitely more care for the education and mental improvement
of all ranks of the people, under the Prussian monarchy
than under the English representative government; and
he held, with the French *Economistes,* that the real security for good government is "un peuple éclairé," which
is not always the fruit of popular institutions, and which
if it could be had without them, would do their work better than they. Though he approved of the Reform Bill,
he predicted what in fact occurred, that it would not produce the great immediate improvements in government
which many expected from it. The men, he said, who could
do these great things did not exist in the country. There
were many points of sympathy between him and me, both

in the new opinions he had adopted and in the old ones which he retained. Like me, he never ceased to be an Utilitarian, and with all his love of the Germans, and enjoyment of their literature, never became in the smallest degree reconciled to the innate-principle metaphysics. He cultivated more and more a kind of German religion, a religion of poetry and feeling with little, if anything, of positive dogma; while, in politics (and here it was that I most differed with him) he acquired an indifference, bordering on contempt, for the progress of popular institutions; though he rejoiced in that of socialism as the most effectual means of compelling the powerful classes to educate the people, and to impress on them the only real means of permanently improving their material condition, a limitation of their numbers. Neither was he, at this time, fundamentally opposed to socialism in itself as an ultimate result of improvement. He professed great disrespect for what he called "the universal principles of human nature of the political economists," and insisted on the evidence which history and daily experience afford of the "extraordinary pliability of human nature" (a phrase which I have somewhere borrowed from him); nor did he think it possible to set any positive bounds to the moral capabilities which might unfold themselves in mankind, under an enlightened direction of social and educational influences. Whether he retained all these opinions to the end of life I know not. Certainly the modes of thinking of his later years, and especially of his last publication, were much more Tory in their general character than those which he held at this time.

My father's tone of thought and feeling I now felt myself at a great distance from; greater, indeed, than a full and calm explanation and reconsideration on both sides might have shown to exist in reality. But my father was not one with whom calm and full explanations on fundamental points of doctrine could be expected, at least with one whom he might consider as, in some sort, a deserter from his standard. Fortunately we were almost always in strong agreement on the political questions of the day, which engrossed a large part of his interest and of his conversation. On those matters of opinion on which we differed, we talked little. He knew that the habit of thinking for myself, which his mode of education had

fostered, sometimes led me to opinions different from his,
and he perceived from time to time that I did not always
tell him *how* different. I expected no good, but only pain
to both of us, from discussing our differences; and I never
expressed them but when he gave utterance to some
opinion or feeling repugnant to mine, in a manner which
would have made it disingenuousness on my part to remain silent.

It remains to speak of what I wrote during these years,
which, independently of my contributions to newspapers,
was considerable. In 1830 and 1831 I wrote the five
essays since published under the title of *Essays on some
Unsettled Questions of Political Economy,* almost as
they now stand, except that in 1833 I partially rewrote the
fifth essay. They were written with no immediate purpose of publication; and when, some years later, I offered
them to a publisher, he declined them. They were only
printed in 1844, after the success of the *System of Logic.*
I also resumed my speculations on this last subject, and
puzzled myself, like others before me, with the great para-
dox of the discovery of new truths by general reasoning.
As to the fact, there could be no doubt. As little could
it be doubted that all reasoning is resolvable into syllogisms,
and that in every syllogism the conclusion is actually contained and implied in the premises. How, being so contained and implied, it could be new truth, and how the
theorems of geometry, so different in appearance from the
definitions and axioms, could be all contained in these,
was a difficulty which no one, I thought, had sufficiently
felt, and which, at all events no one had succeeded in
clearing up. The explanations offered by Whately and
others, though they might give a temporary satisfaction,
always, in my mind, left a mist still hanging over the subject. At last, when reading a second or third time the
chapters on "Reasoning" in the second volume of Dugald
Stewart, interrogating myself on every point, and following out, as far as I knew how, every topic of thought
which the book suggested, I came upon an idea of his
respecting the use of axioms in ratiocination, which I did
not remember to have before noticed, but which now, in
meditating on it, seemed to me not only true of axioms,
but of all general propositions whatever, and to be the
key of the whole perplexity. From this germ grew the

theory of the syllogism propounded in the Second Book of the *Logic;* which I immediately fixed by writing it out. And now, with greatly increased hope of being able to produce a work on logic, of some originality and value, I proceeded to write the First Book, from the rough and imperfect draft I had already made. What I now wrote became the basis of that part of the subsequent treatise; except that it did not contain the theory of kinds, which was a later addition, suggested by otherwise inextricable difficulties which met me in my first attempt to work out the subject of some of the concluding chapters of the Third Book. At the point which I had now reached I made a halt, which lasted five years. I had come to the end of my tether; I could make nothing satisfactory of induction, at this time. I continued to read any book which seemed to promise light on the subject, and appropriated as well as I could, the results; but for a long time I found nothing which seemed to open to me any very important vein of meditation.

In 1832 I wrote several papers for the first series of *Tait's Magazine,* and one for a quarterly periodical called the *Jurist,* which had been founded, and for a short time carried on, by a set of friends, all lawyers and law reformers, with several of whom I was acquainted. The paper in question is the one on the rights and duties of the State respecting corporation and Church property, now standing first among the collected *Dissertations and Discussions;* where one of my articles in *Tait,* "The Currency Juggle," also appears. In the whole mass of what I wrote previous to these, there is nothing of sufficient permanent value to justify reprinting. The paper in the *Jurist,* which I still think a very complete discussion of the rights of the State over foundations, showed both sides of my opinions, asserting as firmly as I should have done at any time the doctrine that all endowments are national property, which the government may and ought to control; but not, as I should once have done, condemning endowments in themselves, and proposing that they should be taken to pay off the national debt. On the contrary, I urged strenuously the importance of having a provision for education, not dependent on the mere demand of the market, that is, on the knowledge and discernment of average parents, but calculated to establish and keep up a higher standard of instruction than is likely to be spontaneously demanded by the buyers of the article. All these opinions have been confirmed and strengthened by the whole course of my subsequent reflections.

CHAPTER VI 1830-1840

COMMENCEMENT OF THE MOST
VALUABLE FRIENDSHIP OF MY LIFE;
MY FATHER'S DEATH; WRITINGS
AND OTHER PROCEEDINGS UP TO
1840

It was at the period of my mental
progress which I have now reached that I formed the
friendship which has been the honour and chief blessing
of my existence, as well as the source of a great part of
all that I have attempted to do, or hope to effect hereafter, for human improvement. My first introduction to
the lady who, after a friendship of twenty years, consented to become my wife, was in 1830, when I was in
my twenty-fifth and she in her twenty-third year. With
her husband's family it was the renewal of an old ac-
quaintanceship. His grandfather lived in the next house
to my father's in Newington Green, and I had, sometimes

when a boy, been invited to play in the old gentleman's garden. He was a fine specimen of the old Scotch Puritan: stern, severe, and powerful, but very kind to children, on whom such men make a lasting impression. Although it was years after my introduction to Mrs. Taylor before my acquaintance with her became at all intimate or confidential, I very soon felt her to be the most admirable person I had ever known. It is not to be supposed that she was, or that any one, at the age at which I first saw her, could be, all that she afterwards became. Least of all could this be true of her, with whom self-improvement, progress in the highest and in all senses, was a law of her nature; a necessity equally from the ardour with which she sought it, and from the spontaneous tendency of faculties which could not receive an impression or an experience without making it the source or the occasion of an accession of wisdom. Up to the time when I first saw her, her rich and powerful nature had chiefly unfolded itself according to the received type of feminine genius. To her outer circle she was a beauty and a wit, with an air of natural distinction felt by all who approached her; to the inner, a woman of deep and strong feeling, of penetrating and intuitive intelligence, and of an eminently meditative and poetic nature. Married at an early age to a most upright, brave, and honourable man, of liberal opinions and good education, but without the intellectual or artistic tastes which would have made him a companion for her, though a steady and affectionate friend, for whom she had true esteem and the strongest affection through life, and whom she most deeply lamented when dead; shut out by the social disabilities of women from any adequate exercise of her highest faculties in action on the world without her life was one of inward meditation, varied by familiar intercourse with a small circle of friends, of whom one only (long since deceased) was a person of genius, or of capabilities of feeling or intellect kindred with her own, but all had more or less of alliance with her in sentiments and opinions. Into this circle I had the good fortune to be admitted, and I soon perceived that she possessed, in combination, the qualities which in all other persons whom I had known I had been only too happy to find singly. In her, complete emancipation from every kind of superstition (including that which attributes a pretended perfection to the order of nature and the universe), and an earnest protest against many things which are still part of the established constitution of society, resulted not from the hard intellect, but from strength of noble and elevated feeling, and co-existed with a highly reverential nature. In general spiritual characteristics, as well as in temperament and organization, I have often compared her, as she was at this time, to Shelley; but in thought and intellect, Shelley, so far as his powers were developed in his short life, was but a child compared with what she ultimately became. Alike in the highest regions of speculation and in the smaller practical concerns of daily life, her mind was the same perfect instrument, piercing to the very heart and marrow of the matter; always seizing the essential idea or principle. The same exactness and rapidity of operation, pervading as it did her sensitive as well as her mental faculties, would, with her gifts of feeling and imagination, have fitted her to be a consummate artist, as her fiery and tender soul and her vigorous eloquence would certainly have made her a great orator, and her profound knowledge of human nature and discernment and sagacity in practical life, would, in the times when such a *carrière* was open to women, have made her eminent among the rulers of mankind. Her intellectual gifts did but minister to a moral character at once the noblest and the best balanced which I have ever met with in life. Her unselfishness was not that of a taught system of duties, but of a heart which thoroughly identified itself with the feelings of others, and often went to excess in consideration for them by imaginatively investing their feelings with the intensity of its own. The passion of justice might have been thought to be her strongest feeling, but for her boundless generosity, and a lovingness ever ready to pour itself forth upon any or all human beings who were capable of giving the smallest feeling in return. The rest of her moral characteristics were such as naturally accompany these qualities of mind and heart: the most genuine modesty combined with the loftiest pride; a simplicity and sincerity which were absolute, towards all who were fit to receive them; the utmost scorn of whatever was mean and cowardly, and a burn-

ing indignation at everything brutal or tyrannical, faith-
less or dishonourable in conduct and character, while
making the broadest distinction between *mala in se* and
mere *mala prohibita*—between acts giving evidence of intrinsic badness in feeling and character, and those which
are only violations of conventions either good or bad,
violations which, whether in themselves right or wrong,
are capable of being committed by persons in every other
respect lovable or admirable.

To be admitted into any degree of mental intercourse
with a being of these qualities could not but have a most
beneficial influence on my development; though the effect
was only gradual, and many years elapsed before her
mental progress and mine went forward in the complete
companionship they at last attained. The benefit I received was far greater than any which I could hope to
give; though to her, who had at first reached her opinions
by the moral intuition of a character of strong feeling,
there was doubtless help as well as encouragement to be
derived from one who had arrived at many of the same
results by study and reasoning; and in the rapidity of her
intellectual growth, her mental activity, which converted
everything into knowledge, doubtless drew from me, as it
did from other sources, many of its materials. What I owe,
even intellectually, to her, is in its detail, almost infinite;
of its general character a few words will give some, though
a very imperfect, idea.

With those who, like all the best and wisest of mankind, are dissatisfied with human life as it is, and whose
feelings are wholly identified with its radical amendment,
there are two main regions of thought. One is the region
of ultimate aims: the constituent elements of the highest
realizable ideal of human life. The other is that of the
immediately useful and practically attainable. In both
these departments, I have acquired more from her teaching than from all other sources taken together. And, to
say truth, it is in these two extremes, principally, that
real certainty lies. My own strength lay wholly in the
uncertain and slippery intermediate region, that of theory,
or moral and political science; respecting the conclusions
of which, in any of the forms in which I have received
or originated them, whether as political economy, analytic
psychology, logic, philosophy of history, or anything else,

it is not the least of my intellectual obligations to her that I have derived from her a wise scepticism, which, while it has not hindered me from following out the honest exercise of my thinking faculties to whatever conclusions might result from it, has put me on my guard against holding or announcing these conclusions with a degree of confidence which the nature of such speculations does not warrant, and has kept my mind not only open to admit, but prompt to welcome and eager to seek, even on the questions on which I have most meditated, any prospect of clearer perceptions and better evidence. I have often received praise, which in my own right I only partially deserve, for the greater practicality which is supposed to be found in my writings, compared with those of most thinkers who have been equally addicted to large generalizations. The writings in which this quality has been observed were not the work of one mind, but of the fusion of two, one of them as pre-eminently practical in its judgments and perceptions of things present as it was high and bold in its anticipations for a remote futurity.

At the present period, however, this influence was only one among many which were helping to shape the character of my future development: and even after it became, I may truly say, the presiding principle of my mental progress, it did not alter the path, but only made me move forward more boldly, and, at the same time, more cautiously, in the same course. The only actual revolution which has ever taken place in my modes of thinking was already complete. My new tendencies had to be confirmed in some respects, moderated in others; but the only substantial changes of opinion that were yet to come related to politics, and consisted, on one hand, in a greater approximation, so far as regards the ultimate prospects of humanity, to a qualified socialism, and on the other, a shifting of my political ideal from pure democracy, as commonly understood by its partizans, to the modified form of it, which is set forth in my *Considerations on Representative Government*.

This last change, which took place very gradually, dates its commencement from my reading, or rather study, of M. de Tocqueville's *Democracy in America*, which fell into my hands immediately after its first appearance. In that remarkable work, the excellences of democracy were pointed out in a more conclusive, because a more specific, manner than I had ever known them to be, even by the most enthusiastic democrats; while the specific dangers which beset democracy, considered as the government of the numerical majority, were brought into equally strong light, and subjected to a masterly analysis, not as reasons for resisting what the author considered as an inevitable result of human progress, but as indications of the weak points of popular government, the defences by which it needs to be guarded, and the correctives which must be added to it in order that while full play is given to its beneficial tendencies, those which are of a different nature may be neutralized or mitigated. I was now well prepared for speculations of this character, and from this time onward my own thoughts moved more and more in the same channel, though the consequent modifications in my practical political creed were spread over many years, as would be shown by comparing my first review of *Democracy in America*, written and published in 1835, with the one in 1840 (reprinted in the *Dissertations*), and this last, with the *Considerations on Representative Government*.

A collateral subject on which also I derived great benefit from the study of Tocqueville was the fundamental question of centralization. The powerful philosophic analysis which he applied to American and to French experience led him to attach the utmost importance to the performance of as much of the collective business of society as can safely be so performed, by the people themselves, without any intervention of the executive government, either to supersede their agency, or to dictate the manner of its exercise. He viewed this practical political activity of the individual citizen not only as one of the most effectual means of training the social feelings and practical intelligence of the people, so important in themselves and so indispensable to good government, but also as the specific counteractive to some of the characteristic infirmities of democracy, and a necessary protection against its degenerating into the only despotism of which, in the modern world, there is real danger—the absolute rule of the head of the executive over a congregation of isolated individuals, all equals but all slaves.

There was, indeed, no immediate peril from this source on the British side of the channel, where nine-tenths of the internal business which elsewhere devolves on the government was transacted by agencies independent of it; where centralization was, and is, the subject not only of rational disapprobation, but of unreasoning prejudice; where jealousy of government interference was a blind feeling preventing or resisting even the most beneficial exertion of legislative authority to correct the abuses of what pretends to be local self-government, but is, too often, selfish mismanagement of local interests, by a jobbing and *borné* local oligarchy. But the more certain the public were to go wrong on the side opposed to centralization, the greater danger was there lest philosophic reformers should fall into the contrary error, and overlook the mischiefs of which they had been spared the painful experience. I was myself, at this very time, actively engaged in defending important measures, such as the great Poor Law Reform of 1834, against an irrational clamour grounded on the anti-centralization prejudice; and had it not been for the lessons of Tocqueville, I do not know that I might not, like many reformers before me, have been hurried into the excess opposite to that, which, being the one prevalent in my own country, it was generally my business to combat. As it is, I have steered carefully between the two errors, and whether I have or have not drawn the line between them exactly in the right place, I have at least insisted with equal emphasis upon the evils on both sides, and have made the means of reconciling the advantages of both a subject of serious study.

In the meanwhile had taken place the election of the first Reformed Parliament, which included several of the most notable of my Radical friends and acquaintances—Grote, Roebuck, Buller, Sir William Molesworth, John and Edward Romilly, and several more; besides Warburton, Strutt, and others, who were in Parliament already. Those who thought themselves, and were called by their friends, the Philosophic Radicals, had now, it seemed, a fair opportunity, in a more advantageous position than they had ever before occupied, for showing what was in them; and I, as well as my father, founded great hopes on them. These hopes were destined to be disappointed. The men were honest, and faithful to their opinions, as far as votes were concerned; often in spite of much discouragement. When measures were proposed, flagrantly at variance with their principles, such as the Irish Coercion Bill, or the Canada Coercion in 1837, they came forward manfully, and braved any amount of hostility and prejudice rather than desert the right. But on the whole they did very little to promote any opinions; they had little enterprise, little activity: they left the lead of the Radical portion of the House to the old hands, to Hume and O'Connell. A partial exception must be made in favour of one or two of the younger men; and in the case of Roebuck, it is his title to permanent remembrance that, in the very first year during which he sat in Parliament, he originated (or re-originated after the unsuccessful attempt of Mr. Brougham) the parliamentary movement for national education; and that he was the first to commence, and for years carried on almost alone, the contest for the self-government of the Colonies. Nothing, on the whole equal to these two things, was done by any other individual, even of those from whom most was expected. And now, on a calm retrospect, I can perceive that the men were less in fault than we supposed, and that we had expected too much from them. They were in unfavourable circumstances. Their lot was cast in the ten years of inevitable reaction, when, the Reform excitement being over, and the few legislative improvements which the public really called for having been rapidly effected, power gravitated back in its natural direction to those who were for keeping things as they were; when the public mind desired rest, and was less disposed than at any other period since the peace to let itself be moved by attempts to work up the Reform feeling into fresh activity in favour of new things. It would have required a great political leader, which no one is to be blamed for not being, to have effected really great things by parliamentary discussion when the nation was in this mood. My father and I had hoped that some competent leader might arise; some man of philosophic attainments and popular talents, who could have put heart into the many younger or less distinguished men that would have been ready to join him—could have made them available, to the extent of their talents, in bringing advanced ideas before the public—could have used the House of Commons as a rostrum or a teacher's chair for instructing and impelling the public mind; and would either have forced the Whigs to receive their measures from him, or have taken the lead of the Reform party out of their hands. Such a leader there would have been, if my father had been in Parliament. For want of such a man, the instructed Radicals sank into a mere *Côté Gauche* of the Whig party. With a keen, and as I now think, an exaggerated sense of the possibilities which were open to the Radicals if they made even ordinary exertion for their opinions, I laboured from this time till 1839, both by personal influence with some of them, and by writings, to put ideas into their heads, and purpose into their hearts. I did some good with Charles Buller, and some with Sir William Molesworth; both of whom did valuable service, but were unhappily cut off almost in the beginning of their usefulness. On the whole, however, my attempt was vain. To have had a chance of succeeding in it, required a different position from mine. It was a task only for one who, being himself in Parliament, could have mixed with the Radical members in daily consultation, could himself have taken the initiative, and instead of urging others to lead, could have summoned them to follow.

What I could do by writing, I did. During the year 1833 I continued working in the *Examiner* with Fonblanque, who at that time was zealous in keeping up the fight for radicalism against the Whig Ministry. During the session of 1834 I wrote comments on passing events, of the nature of newspaper articles (under the title of "Notes on the Newspapers"), in the *Monthly Repository,* a magazine conducted by Mr. Fox, well known as a preacher and political orator, and subsequently as member of Parliament for Oldham; with whom I had lately become acquainted, and for whose sake chiefly I wrote in his magazine. I contributed several other articles to this periodical, the most considerable of which (on the theory of poetry), is reprinted in the *Dissertations*. Altogether, the writings (independently of those in newspapers) which I published from 1832 to 1834, amount to a large volume. This, however, includes abstracts of several of Plato's *Dialogues,* with introductory remarks, which, though not published until 1834, had been written several years earlier; and which I afterwards, on various occasions, found to have been read, and their authorship known, by more people than were aware of anything else which I had written, up to that time. To complete the tale of my writings at this period, I may add that in 1833, at the request of Bulwer, who was just then completing his *England and the English* (a work, at that time, greatly in advance of the public mind), I wrote for him a critical account of Bentham's philosophy, a small part of which he incorporated in his text, and printed the rest (with an honourable acknowledgement), as an appendix. In this, along with the favourable, a part also of the unfavourable side of my estimation of Bentham's doctrines, considered as a complete philosophy, was for the first time put into print.

But an opportunity soon offered, by which, as it seemed, I might have it in my power to give more effectual aid, and, at the same time, stimulus, to the Philosophic Radical party, than I had done hitherto. One of the projects occasionally talked of between my father and me, and some of the parliamentary and other Radicals who frequented his house, was the foundation of a periodical organ of philosophic radicalism to take the place which the *Westminster Review* had been intended to fill; and the scheme had gone so far as to bring under discussion the pecuniary contributions which could be looked for, and the choice of an editor. Nothing, however, came of it for some time; but in the summer of 1834 Sir William Molesworth, himself a laborious student, and a precise and metaphysical thinker, capable of aiding the cause by his pen as well as by his purse, spontaneously proposed to establish a review, provided I would consent to be the real, if I could not be the ostensible, editor. Such a proposal was not to be refused; and the review was founded, at first under the title of the *London Review,* and afterwards under that of the *London and Westminster,* Molesworth having bought the *Westminster* from its proprietor, General Thompson, and merged the two into one. In the years between 1834 and 1840 the conduct of this *Review* occupied the greater part of my spare time. In the beginning, it did not, as a whole, by any means represent my opinions. I was under the necessity of conceding much to my inevitable associates. The *Review* was established to be the representative of the Philosophic Radicals, with most of whom I was now at issue on many essential points, and among whom

I could not even claim to be the most important individual. My father's co-operation as a writer we all deemed indispensable, and he wrote largely in it until prevented by his last illness. The subjects of his articles, and the strength and decision with which his opinions were expressed in them, made the *Review* at first derive its tone and colouring from him much more than from any of the other writers. I could not exercise editorial control over his articles, and I was sometimes obliged to sacrifice to him portions of my own. The old *Westminster Review* doctrines, but little modified, thus formed the staple of the *Review;* but I hoped, by the side of these, to introduce other ideas and another tone, and to obtain for my own shade of opinion a fair representation, along with those of other members of the party. With this end chiefly in view, I made it one of the peculiarities of the work that every article should bear an initial, or some other signature, and be held to express the opinions solely of the individual writer; the editor being only responsible for its being worth publishing, and not in conflict with the objects for which the *Review* was set on foot. I had an opportunity of putting in practice my scheme of conciliation between the old and the new philosophic radicalism by the choice of a subject for my own first contribution. Professor Sedgwick, a man of eminence in a particular walk of natural science, but who should not have trespassed into philosophy, had lately published his *Discourse on the Studies of Cambridge,* which had as its most prominent feature an intemperate assault on analytic psychology and Utilitarian ethics, in the form of an attack on Locke and Paley. This had excited great indignation in my father and others, which I thought it fully deserved. And here, I imagined, was an opportunity of at the same time repelling an unjust attack, and inserting into my defence of Hartleianism and utilitarianism a number of the opinions which constituted my view of those subjects, as distinguished from that of my old associates. In this I partially succeeded, though my relation to my father would have made it painful to me in any case, and impossible in a review for which he wrote, to speak out my whole mind on the subject at this time.

I am, however, inclined to think that my father was not so much opposed as he seemed, to the modes of thought in which I believed myself to differ from him; that he did injustice to his own opinions by the unconscious exaggerations of an intellect emphatically polemical; and that when thinking without an adversary in view, he was willing to make room for a great portion of the truths he seemed to deny. I have frequently observed that he made large allowance in practice for considerations which seemed to have no place in his theory. His *Fragment on Mackintosh,* which he wrote and published about this time, although I greatly admired some parts of it, I read as a whole with more pain than pleasure; yet on reading it again, long after, I found little in the opinions it contains, but what I think in the main just; and I can even sympathize in his disgust at the *verbiage* of Mackintosh, though his asperity towards it went not only beyond what was judicious, but beyond what was even fair. One thing, which I thought, at the time, of good augury, was the very favourable reception he gave to Tocqueville's *Democracy in America.* It is true, he said and thought much more about what Tocqueville said in favour of democracy than about what he said of its disadvantages. Still, his high appreciation of a book which was at any rate an example of a mode of treating the question of government almost the reverse of his—wholly inductive and analytical, instead of purely ratiocinative—gave me great encouragement. He also approved of an article which I published in the first number following the junction of the two reviews, the essay reprinted in the *Dissertations,* under the title "Civilization"; into which I threw many of my new opinions, and criticized rather emphatically the mental and moral tendencies of the time, on grounds and in a manner which I certainly had not learnt from him.

All speculation, however, on the possible future developments of my fathers' opinions, and on the probabilities of permanent co-operation between him and me in the promulgation of our thoughts, was doomed to be cut short. During the whole of 1835 his health had been declining; his symptoms became unequivocally those of pulmonary consumption, and after lingering to the last stage of debility, he died on the twenty-third of June, 1836. Until the last few days of his life there was no apparent abatement of intellectual vigour; his interest in all things and persons that had interested him through life was undiminished, nor did the approach of death cause the smallest wavering (as in so strong and firm a mind it was impossible that it should) in his convictions on the subject of religion. His principal satisfaction, after he knew that his end was near, seemed to be the thought of what he had done to make the world better than he found it; and his chief regret in not living longer, that he had not had time to do more.

His place is an eminent one in the literary, and even in the political history of his country; and it is far from honourable to the generation which has benefited by his worth that he is so seldom mentioned, and, compared with men far his inferiors, so little remembered. This is probably to be ascribed mainly to two causes. In the first place, the thought of him merges too much in the deservedly superior fame of Bentham. Yet he was anything but Bentham's mere follower or disciple. Precisely because he was himself one of the most original thinkers of his time, he was one of the earliest to appreciate and adopt the most important mass of original thought which had been produced by the generation preceding him. His mind and Bentham's were essentially of different construction. He had not all Bentham's high qualities, but neither had Bentham all his. It would, indeed, be ridiculous to claim for him the praise of having accomplished for mankind such splendid services as Bentham's. He did not revolutionize, or rather create, one of the great departments of human thought. But, leaving out of the reckoning all that portion of his labours in which he benefited by what Bentham had done, and counting only what he achieved in a province in which Bentham had done nothing, that of analytic psychology, he will be known to posterity as one of the greatest names in that most important branch of speculation, on which all the moral and political sciences ultimately rest, and will mark one of the essential stages in its progress. The other reason which has made his fame less than he deserved, is that notwithstanding the great number of his opinions which, partly through his own efforts, have now been generally adopted, there was, on the whole, a marked opposition between his spirit and that of the present time. As Brutus was called the last of the Romans, so was he the last of the eighteenth century: he continued its tone of thought and sentiment into the nineteenth (though not unmodified nor unimproved), partaking neither in the good nor in the bad influences of the reaction against the eighteenth century, which was the great characteristic of the first half of the nineteenth. The eighteenth century was a great age, an age of strong and brave men, and he was a fit companion for its strongest and bravest. By his writings and his personal influence he was a great centre of light to his generation. During his later years he was quite as much the head and leader of the intellectual Radicals in England as Voltaire was of the *philosophes* of France. It is only one of his minor merits, that he was the originator of all sound statesmanship in regard to the subject of his largest work, India. He wrote on no subject which he did not enrich with valuable thought, and excepting the *Elements of Political Economy,* a very useful book when first written, but which has now for some time finished its work, it will be long before any of his books will be wholly superseded, or will cease to be instructive reading to students of their subjects. In the power of influencing, by mere force of mind and character, the convictions and purposes of others, and in the strenuous exertion of that power to promote freedom and progress, he left, as my knowledge extends, no equal among men, and but one among women.

Though acutely sensible of my own inferiority in the qualities by which he acquired his personal ascendancy, I had now to try what it might be possible for me to accomplish without him; and the *Review* was the instrument on which I built my chief hopes of establishing a useful influence over the liberal and democratic section of the public mind. Deprived of my father's aid, I was also exempted from the restraints and reticences by which that aid had been purchased. I did not feel that there was any other Radical writer or politician to whom I was bound to defer, further than consisted with my own opinions; and having the complete confidence of Molesworth, I resolved henceforth to give full scope to my own opinions and modes of thought, and to open the Review widely to all writers who were in sympathy with progress as I understood it, even though I should lose by it the support of my former associates. Carlyle, consequently, became from this time a frequent writer in the *Review;*

Sterling, soon after, an occasional one; and though each individual article continued to be the expression of the private sentiments of its writer, the general tone conformed in some tolerable degree to my opinions. For the conduct of the Review, under, and in conjunction with me, I associated with myself a young Scotchman of the name of Robertson, who had some ability and information, much industry, and an active scheming head, full of devices for making the Review more saleable, and on whose capacities in that direction I founded a good deal of hope; insomuch that when Molesworth, in the beginning of 1837, became tired of carrying on the *Review* at a loss, and desirous of getting rid of it (he had done his part honourably, and at no small pecuniary cost), I, very imprudently for my own pecuniary interest, and very much from reliance on Robertson's devices, determined to continue it at my own risk until his plans should have had a fair trial. The devices were good, and I never had any reason to change my opinion of them. But I do not believe that any devices would have made a Radical and Democratic review defray its expenses, including a paid editor or sub-editor, and a liberal payment to writers. I myself and several frequent contributors gave our labour gratuitously, as we had done for Molesworth; but the paid contributors continued to be remunerated on the usual scale of the *Edinburgh* and *Quarterly Reviews;* and this could not be done from the proceeds of the sale.

In the same year, 1837, and in the midst of these occupations, I resumed the *Logic*. I had not touched my pen on the subject for five years, having been stopped and brought to a halt on the threshold of induction. I had gradually discovered that what was mainly wanting, to overcome the difficulties of that branch of the subject, was a comprehensive, and, at the same time, accurate view of the whole circle of physical science, which I feared it would take me a long course of study to acquire; since I knew not of any book, or other guide, that would spread out before me the generalities and processes of the sciences, and I apprehended that I should have no choice but to extract them for myself, as I best could, from the details. Happily for me, Dr. Whewell, early in this year, published his *History of the Inductive Sciences*. I read it with eagerness, and found in it a considerable approximation to what I wanted. Much, if not most, of the philosophy of the work appeared open to objection; but the materials were there, for my own thoughts to work upon; and the author had given to those materials that first degree of elaboration which so greatly facilitates and abridges the subsequent labour. I had now obtained what I had been waiting for. Under the impulse given me by the thoughts excited by Dr. Whewell, I read again Sir J. Herschel's *Discourse on the Study of Natural Philosophy;* and I was able to measure the progress my mind had made by the great help I now found in this work— though I had read and even reviewed it several years before with little profit. I now set myself vigorously to work out the subject in thought and in writing. The time I bestowed on this had to be stolen from occupations more urgent. I had just two months to spare, at this period, in the intervals of writing for the *Review.* In these two months I completed the first draft of about a third, the most difficult third, of the book. What I had before written I estimate at another third, so that only one-third remained. What I wrote at this time consisted of the remainder of the doctrine of reasoning (the theory of trains of reasoning, and demonstrative science), and the greater part of the Book on induction. When this was done, I had, as it seemed to me, untied all the really hard knots, and the completion of the book had become only a question of time. Having got thus far, I had to leave off in order to write two articles for the next number of the *Review.* When these were written, I returned to the subject, and now for the first time fell in with the two volumes of it which were all that had at that time been published.

My theory of induction was substantially completed before I knew of Comte's book; and it is perhaps well that I came to it by a different road from his, since the consequence has been that my treatise contains what his certainly does not, a reduction of the inductive process to strict rules and to a scientific test, such as the syllogism is for ratiocination. Comte is always precise and profound on the method of investigation, but he does not even attempt any exact definition of the conditions of proof; and his writings show that he never attained a just conception of them. This, however, was specifically the problem which, in treating of induction, I had proposed to

myself. Nevertheless, I gained much from Comte, with
which to enrich my chapters in the subsequent rewriting;
and his book was of essential service to me in some of
the parts which still remained to be thought out. As his
subsequent volumes successively made their appearance,
I read them with avidity, but, when he reached the subject
of social science, with varying feelings. The fourth volume
disappointed me: it contained those of his opinions on
social subjects with which I most disagree. But the fifth,
containing the connected view of history, rekindled all
my enthusiasm; which the sixth (or concluding) volume
did not materially abate. In a merely logical point of
view, the only leading conception for which I am indebted
to him is that of the inverse deductive method, as the one
chiefly applicable to the complicated subjects of history
and statistics: a process differing from the more common
form of the deductive method in this—that instead of
arriving at its conclusions by general reasoning, and veri-
fying them by specific experience (as is the natural order
in the deductive branches of physical science), it obtains
its generalizations by a collection of specific experience,
and verifies them by ascertaining whether they are such
as would follow from known general principles. This was
an idea entirely new to me when I found it in Comte;
and but for him I might not soon (if ever) have arrived
at it.

I had been long an ardent admirer of Comte's writings
before I had any communication with himself; nor did
I ever, to the last, see him in the body. But for some
years we were frequent correspondents, until our correspondence became controversial, and our zeal cooled. I
was the first to slacken correspondence; he was the first
to drop it. I found, and he probably found likewise, that
I could do no good to his mind, and that all the good he
could do to mine he did by his books. This would never
have led to discontinuance of intercourse if the difference
between us had been on matters of simple doctrine. But
they were chiefly on those points of opinion which blended
in both of us with our strongest feelings, and determined
the entire direction of our aspirations. I had fully agreed
with him when he maintained that the mass of mankind,
including even their rulers in all the practical departments of life, must, from the necessity of the case,

accept most of their opinions on political and social matters, as they do on physical, from the authority of those who have bestowed more study on those subjects than they generally have it in their power to do. This lesson had been strongly impressed on me by the early work of Comte, to which I have adverted. And there was nothing in his great treatise which I admired more than his remarkable exposition of the benefits which the nations of modern Europe have historically derived from the separation, during the Middle Ages, of temporal and spiritual power, and the distinct organization of the latter. I agreed with him that the moral and intellectual ascendancy, once exercised by priests, must in time pass into the hands of philosophers, and will naturally do so when they become sufficiently unanimous, and in other respects worthy to possess it. But when he exaggerated this line of thought into a practical system in which philosophers were to be organized into a kind of corporate hierarchy, invested wtih almost the same spiritual supremacy (though without any secular power) once possessed by the Catholic Church; when I found him relying on this spiritual authority as the only security for good government, the sole bulwark against practical oppression, and expecting that by it a system of despotism in the state and despotism in the family would be rendered innocuous and beneficial it is not surprising, that while as logicians we were nearly at one, as sociologists we could travel together no further. M. Comte lived to carry out these doctrines to their extremest consequences, by planning, in his last work, the *Système de Politique Positive,* the completest system of spiritual and temporal despotism which ever yet emanated from a human brain, unless possibly that of Ignatius Loyola: a system by which the yoke of general opinion, wielded by an organized body of spiritual teachers and rulers, would be made supreme over every action, and as far as is in human possibility, every thought, of every member of the community, as well in the things which regard only himself as in those which concern the interests of others. It is but just to say that this work is a considerable improvement, in many points of feeling, over Comte's previous writings on the same subjects; but as an accession to social philosophy, the only value it seems to me to possess consists in putting an end to the notion that no effectual moral authority can be maintained over society without the aid of religious belief; for Comte's work recognizes no religion except that of humanity, yet it leaves an irresistible conviction that any moral beliefs concurred in by the community generally may be brought to bear upon the whole conduct and lives of its individual members, with an energy and potency truly alarming to think of. The book stands a monumental warning to thinkers on society and politics of what happens when once men lose sight in their speculations of the value of liberty and of individuality.

To return to myself. The *Review* engrossed, for some time longer, nearly all the time I could devote to authorship, or to thinking with authorship in view. The articles from the *London and Westminster Review* which are reprinted in the *Dissertations* are scarcely a fourth part of those I wrote. In the conduct of the *Review* I had two principal objects. One was to free philosophic radicalism from the reproach of sectarian Benthamism. I desired, while retaining the precision of expression, the definiteness of meaning, the contempt of declamatory phrases and vague generalities, which were so honourably characteristic both of Bentham and of my father, to give a wider basis and a more free and genial character to Radical speculations; to show that there was a Radical philosophy, better and more complete than Bentham's, while recognizing and incorporating all of Bentham's which is permanently valuable. In this first object I, to a certain extent, succeeded. The other thing I attempted, was to stir up the educated Radicals, in and out of Parliament, to exertion, and induce them to make themselves what I thought by using the proper means they might become— a powerful party capable of taking the government of the country, or at least of dictating the terms on which they should share it with the Whigs. This attempt was from the first chimerical: partly because the time was unpropitious, the Reform fervour being in its period of ebb, and the Tory influences powerfully rallying; but still more, because, as Austin so truly said, "the country did not contain the men." Among the Radicals in Parliament there were several qualified to be useful members of an enlightened Radical party, but none capable of forming and leading such a party. The exhortations I addressed to them found no response. One occasion did present itself when there seemed to be room for a bold and successful stroke for radicalism. Lord Durham had left the Ministry, by reason, as was thought, of their not being sufficiently Liberal; he afterwards accepted from them the task of ascertaining and removing the causes of the Canadian rebellion; he had shown a disposition to surround himself at the outset with Radical advisers; one of his earliest measures, a good measure both in intention and in effect, having been disapproved and reversed by the Government at home, he had resigned his post, and placed himself openly in a position of quarrel with the Ministers. Here was a possible chief for a Radical party in the person of a man of importance, who was hated by the Tories and had just been injured by the Whigs. Any one who had the most elementary notions of party tactics must have attempted to make something of such an opportunity. Lord Durham was bitterly attacked from all sides, inveighed against by enemies, given up by timid friends; while those who would willingly have defended him did not know what to say. He appeared to be returning a defeated and discredited man. I had followed the Canadian events from the beginning; I had been one of the prompters of his prompters; his policy was almost exactly what mine would have been, and I was in a position to defend it. I wrote and published a manifesto in the *Review*, in which I took the very highest ground in his behalf, claiming for him not mere acquittal, but praise and honour. Instantly a number of other writers took up the tone: I believe there was a portion of truth in what Lord Durham, soon after, with polite exaggeration, said to me—that to this article might be ascribed the almost triumphal reception which he met with on his arrival in England. I believe it to have been the word in season, which, at a critical moment, does much to decide the result; the touch which determines whether a stone, set in motion at the top of an eminence, shall roll down on one side or on the other. All hopes connected with Lord Durham as a politician soon vanished; but with regard to Canadian, and generally to colonial policy, the cause was gained: Lord Durham's report, written by Charles Buller, partly under the inspiration of Wakefield, began a new era; its recommendations, extending to complete internal self-government, were in full operation in Canada within two or three years, and have been since extended to nearly all the other colonies, of European race, which have any claim to the character of important communities. And I may say that in successfully upholding the reputation of Lord Durham and his advisers at the most important moment, I contributed materially to this result.

One other case occurred during my conduct of the Review, which similarly illustrated the effect of taking a prompt initiative. I believe that the early success and reputation of Carlyle's *French Revolution,* were considerably accelerated by what I wrote about it in the *Review.* Immediately on its publication, and before the commonplace critics, all whose rules and modes of judgement it set at defiance, had time to preoccupy the public with their disapproval of it, I wrote and published a review of the book, hailing it as one of those productions of genius which are above all rules, and are a law to themselves. Neither in this case nor in that of Lord Durham do I ascribe the impression, which I think was produced by what I wrote, to any particular merit of execution; indeed, in at least one of the cases (the article on Carlyle) I do not think the execution was good. And in both instances, I am persuaded that anybody, in a position to be read, who had expressed the same opinion at the same precise time, and had made any tolerable statement of the just grounds for it, would have produced the same effect. But, after the complete failure of my hopes of putting a new life into Radical politics by means of the *Review,* I am glad to look back on those two instances of success in an honest attempt to do immediate service to things and persons that deserved it.

After the last hope of the formation of a Radical party had disappeared, it was time for me to stop the heavy expenditure of time and money which the *Review* cost me. It had to some extent answered my personal purpose as a vehicle for my opinions. It had enabled me to express in print much of my altered mode of thought, and to separate myself in a marked manner from the narrower Benthamism of my early writings. This was done by the general tone of all I wrote, including various purely literary articles, but especially by the two papers (reprinted in

the *Dissertations*) which attempted a philosophical estimate of Bentham and of Coleridge. In the first of these,
while doing full justice to the merits of Bentham, I pointed
out what I thought the errors and deficiencies of his
philosophy. The substance of this criticism I still think
perfectly just; but I have sometimes doubted whether it
was right to publish it at that time. I have often felt that
Bentham's philosophy, as an instrument of progress, has
been to some extent discredited before it had done its
work, and that to lend a hand towards lowering its
reputation was doing more harm than service to improvement. Now, however, when a counter-reaction appears to
be setting in towards what is good in Benthamism, I can
look with more satisfaction on this criticism of its defects,
especially as I have myself balanced it by vindications
of the fundamental principles of Bentham's philosophy,
which are reprinted along with it in the same collection.
In the essay on Coleridge I attempted to characterize the
European reaction against the negative philosophy of
the eighteenth century; and here, if the effect only of this
one paper were to be considered, I might be thought to
have erred by giving undue prominence to the favourable
side, as I had done in the case of Bentham to the unfavourable. In both cases, the impetus with which I had detached
myself from what was untenable in the doctrines of
Bentham and of the eighteenth century may have carried me, though in appearance rather than in reality, too
far on the contrary side. But as far as relates to the
article on Coleridge, my defence is that I was writing
for Radicals and Liberals, and it was my business to
dwell most on that, in writers of a different school, from
the knowledge of which they might derive most improvement.

The number of the *Review* which contained the paper
on Coleridge was the last which was published during my
proprietorship. In the spring of 1840 I made over the
Review to Mr. Hickson, who had been a frequent and
very useful unpaid contributor under my management;
only stipulating that the change should be marked by a
resumption of the old name, that of *Westminster Review.*
Under that name Mr. Hickson conducted it for ten years,
on the plan of dividing among contributors only the net
proceeds of the *Review,* giving his own labour as writer

and editor gratuitously. Under the difficulty in obtaining writers, which arose from this low scale of payment, it is highly creditable to him that he was able to maintain, in some tolerable degree, the character of the *Review* as an organ of radicalism and progress. I did not cease altogether to write for the *Review,* but continued to send it occasional contributions, not, however, exclusively; for the greater circulation of the *Edinburgh Review* induced me from this time to offer articles to it also when I had anything to say for which it appeared to be a suitable vehicle. And the concluding volumes of *Democracy in America,* having just then come out, I inaugurated myself as a contributor to the *Edinburgh,* by the article on that work, which heads the second volume of the *Dissertations.*

CHAPTER VII 1840-1870

GENERAL VIEW OF THE REMAINDER
OF MY LIFE: COMPLETION OF THE
System of Logic; PUBLICATION OF THE
Principles of Political Economy; MAR‑
RIAGE; RETIREMENT FROM THE IN‑
DIA HOUSE; PUBLICATION OF *Liberty,
Considerations on Representative Gov‑
ernment;* CIVIL WAR IN AMERICA; *Ex‑
amination of Sir William Hamilton's
Philosophy;* PARLIAMENTARY LIFE

From this time, what is worth relating
of my life will come into a very small compass; for I have
no further mental changes to tell of, but only, as I hope,
a continued mental progress; which does not admit of a
consecutive history, and the results of which, if real, will
be best found in my writings. I shall, therefore, greatly
abridge the chronicle of my subsequent years.

The first use I made of the leisure which I gained by disconnecting myself from the *Review* was to finish the *Logic*. In July and August, 1838, I had found an interval in which to execute what was still undone of the original draft of the Third Book. In working out the logical theory of those laws of nature which are not laws of causation, nor corollaries from such laws, I was led to recognize kinds as realities in nature, and not mere distinctions for convenience; a light which I had not obtained when the First Book was written, and which made it necessary for me to modify and enlarge several chapters of that Book. The Book on "Language and Classification," and the chapter on the "Classification of Fallacies" were drafted in the autumn of the same year; the remainder of the work, in the summer and autumn of 1840. From April following, to the end of 1841, my spare time was devoted to a complete rewriting of the book from its commencement. It is in this way that all my books have been composed. They were always written at least twice over; a first draft of the entire work was completed to the very end of the subject, then the whole begun again *de novo;* but incorporating, in the second writing, all sentences and parts of sentences of the old draft which appeared as suitable to my purpose as anything which I could write in lieu of them. I have found great advantages in this system of double redaction. It combines, better than any other mode of composition, the freshness and vigour of the first conception with the superior precision and completeness resulting from prolonged thought. In my own case, moreover, I have found that the patience necessary for a careful elaboration of the details of composition and expression costs much less effort after the entire subject has been once gone through, and the substance of all that I find to say has in some manner, however imperfect, been got upon paper. The only thing which I am careful, in the first draft, to make as perfect as I am able, is the arrangement. If that is bad, the whole thread on which the ideas string themselves becomes twisted: thoughts placed in a wrong connexion are not expounded in a manner that suits the right, and a first draft with this original vice is next to useless as a foundation for the final treatment.

During the rewriting of the *Logic,* Dr. Whewell's *Phi-*

losophy of the Inductive Sciences made its appearance; a circumstance fortunate for me, as it gave me what I greatly desired, a full treatment of the subject by an antagonist, and enabled me to present my ideas with greater clearness and emphasis as well as fuller and more varied development, in defending them against definite objections, or confronting them distinctly with an opposite theory. The controversies with Dr. Whewell, as well as much matter derived from Comte, were first introduced into the book in the course of the rewriting.

At the end of 1841, the book being ready for the press, I offered it to Murray, who kept it until too late for publication that season, and then refused it, for reasons which could just as well have been given at first. But I have had no cause to regret a rejection which led to my offering it to Mr. Parker, by whom it was published in the spring of 1843. My original expectations of success were extremely limited. Archbishop Whately had, indeed, rehabilitated the name of logic, and the study of the forms, rules, and fallacies of ratiocination; and Dr. Whewell's writings had begun to excite an interest in the other part of my subject, the theory of induction. A treatise, however, on a matter so abstract could not be expected to be popular; it could only be a book for students, and students on such subjects were not only (at least in England) few, but addicted chiefly to the opposite school of metaphysics, the ontological and "innate principles" school. I therefore did not expect that the book would have many readers, or approvers; and looked for little practical effect from it, save that of keeping the tradition unbroken of what I thought a better philosophy. What hopes I had of exciting any immediate attention were mainly grounded on the polemical propensities of Dr. Whewell; who, I thought, from observation of his conduct in other cases, would probably do something to bring the book into notice, by replying, and that promptly, to the attack on his opinions. He did reply, but not till 1850, just in time for me to answer him in the third edition. How the book came to have, for a work of the kind, so much success, and what sort of persons compose the bulk of those who have bought, I will not venture to say read, it, I have never thoroughly understood. But taken in conjunction with the many proofs which have since been given of a revival of speculation, speculation too of a free kind, in many quarters, and above all (where at one time I should have least expected it) in the universities, the fact becomes partially intelligible. I have never indulged the illusion that the book had made any considerable impression on philosophical opinion. The German, or a priori view of human knowledge, and of the knowing faculties, is likely for some time longer (though it may be hoped in a diminishing degree) to predominate among those who occupy themselves with such inquiries, both here and on the Continent. But the *System of Logic* supplies what was much wanted, a text-book of the opposite doctrine—that which derives all knowledge from experience, and all moral and intellectual qualities principally from the direction given to the associations. I make as humble an estimate as anybody of what either an analysis of logical processes, or any possible canons of evidence, can do by themselves towards guiding or rectifying the operations of the understanding. Combined with other requisites, I certainly do think them of great use; but whatever may be the practical value of a true philosophy of these matters, it is hardly possible to exaggerate the mischiefs of a false one. The notion that truths external to the mind may be known by intuition or consciousness, independently of observation and experience, is, I am persuaded, in these times, the great intellectual support of false doctrines and bad institutions. By the aid of this theory, every inveterate belief and every intense feeling, of which the origin is not remembered, is enabled to dispense with the obligation of justifying itself by reason, and is erected into its own all-sufficient voucher and justification. There never was such an instrument devised for consecrating all deep-seated prejudices. And the chief strength of this false philosophy in morals, politics, and religion lies in the appeal which it is accustomed to make to the evidence of mathematics and of the cognate branches of physical science. To expel it from these is to drive it from its stronghold; and because this had never been effectually done, the intuitive school, even after what my father had written in his *Analysis of the Mind,* had in appearance, and as far as published writings were concerned, on the whole best of the argument. In attempting to clear up the real nature of the evidence of

mathematical and physical truths, the *System of Logic* met
the intuitive philosophers on ground on which they had
previously been deemed unassailable; and gave its own
explanation, from experience and association, of that peculiar character of what are called necessary truths, which
is adduced as proof that their evidence must come from
a deeper source than experience. Whether this has been
done effectually, is still *sub judice;* and even then, to
deprive a mode of thought so strongly rooted in human
prejudices and partialities of its mere speculative support
goes but a very little way towards overcoming it; but
though only a step, it is a quite indispensable one; for
since, after all, prejudice can only be successful combated
by philosophy, no way can really be made against it
permanently until it has been shown not to have philosophy on its side.

Being now released from any active concern in temporary politics, and from any literary occupation involving
personal communication with contributors and others, I
was enabled to indulge the inclination, natural to thinking
persons when the age of boyish vanity is once past, for
limiting my own society to a very few persons. General
society, as now carried on in England, is so insipid an
affair, even to the persons who make it what it is, that it is
kept up for any reason rather than the pleasure it affords.
All serious discussion on matters on which opinions differ
being considered ill-bred, and the national deficiency in
liveliness and sociability having prevented the cultivation
of the art of talking agreeably on trifles, in which the
French of the last century so much excelled, the sole
attraction of what is called society to those who are not
at the top of the tree is the hope of being aided to climb
a little higher in it; while to those who are already at the
top, it is chiefly a compliance with custom, and with the
supposed requirements of their station. To a person of any
but a very common order in thought or feeling, such
society, unless he has personal objects to serve by it,
must be supremely unattractive; and most people, in
the present day, of any really high class of intellect,
make their contact with it so slight, and at such long
intervals, as to be almost considered as retiring from it
altogether. Those persons of any mental superiority who
do otherwise are, almost without exception, greatly de-

teriorated by it. Not to mention loss of time, the tone of
their feelings is lowered: they become less in earnest
about those of their opinions respecting which they must
remain silent in the society they frequent; they come to
look upon their most elevated objects as unpractical,
or, at least, too remote from realization to be more than
a vision, or a theory; and if, more fortunate than most,
they retain their higher principles unimpaired, yet with
respect to the persons and affairs of their own day they
insensibly adopt the modes of feeling and judgement in
which they can hope for sympathy from the company they
keep. A person of high intellect should never go into
unintellectual society unless he can enter it as an apostle;
yet he is the only person with high objects who can safely
enter it at all. Persons even of intellectual aspirations had
much better, if they can, make their habitual associates
of at least their equals, and, as far as possible, their
superiors in knowledge, intellect, and elevation of sentiment. Moreover, if the character is formed, and the mind
made up on the few cardinal points of human opinion,
agreement of conviction and feeling on these has been
felt in all times to be an essential requisite of anything
worthy the name of friendship, in a really earnest mind.
All these circumstances united made the number very
small of those whose society, and still more whose intimacy, I now voluntarily sought.

Among these, the principal was the incomparable friend
of whom I have already spoken. At this period she lived
mostly with one young daughter, in a quiet part of the
country, and only occasionally in town, with her first
husband, Mr. Taylor. I visited her equally in both places;
and was greatly indebted to the strength of character
which enabled her to disregard the false interpretations
liable to be put on the frequency of my visits to her while
living generally apart from Mr. Taylor, and on our
occasionally travelling together, though in all other respects
our conduct during those years gave not the slightest
ground for any other supposition than the true one, that
our relation to each other at that time was one of strong
affection and confidential intimacy only. For though we
did not consider the ordinances of society binding on a
subject so entirely personal, we did feel bound that our

conduct should be such as in no degree to bring discredit on her husband, nor therefore on herself.

In this third period (as it may be termed) of my mental progress, which now went hand in hand with hers, my opinions gained equally in breadth and depth, I understood more things, and those which I had understood before, I now understood more thoroughly. I had now completely turned back from what there had been of excess in my reaction against Benthamism. I had, at the height of that reaction, certainly become much more indulgent to the common opinions of society and the world, and more willing to be content with seconding the superficial improvement which had begun to take place in those common opinions than became one whose convictions, on so many points, differed fundamentally from them. I was much more inclined than I can now approve to put in abeyance the more decidedly heretical part of my opinions, which I now look upon as almost the only ones the assertion of which tends in any way to regenerate society. But in addition to this, our opinions were far *more* heretical than mine had been in the days of my most extreme Benthamism. In those days I had seen little further than the old school of political economists into the possibilities of fundamental improvement in social arrangements. Private property, as now understood, and inheritance, appeared to me, as to them, the *dernier mot* of legislation; and I looked no further than to mitigating the inequalities consequent on these institutions, by getting rid of primogeniture and entails. The notion that it was possible to go further than this in removing the injustice—for injustice it is, whether admitting of a complete remedy or not—involved in the fact that some are born to riches and the vast majority to poverty, I then reckoned chimerical, and only hoped that by universal education, leading to voluntary restraint on population, the portion of the poor might be made more tolerable. In short, I was a democrat, but not the least of a socialist. We were now much less democrats than I had been, because so long as education continues to be so wretchedly imperfect we dreaded the ignorance and especially the selfishness and brutality of the mass; but our ideal of ultimate improvement went far beyond democracy, and would class us decidedly under the general designation of social-

ists. While we repudiated with the greatest energy that
tyranny of society over the individual which most socialistic systems are supposed to involve, we yet looked forward to a time when society will no longer be divided into
the idle and the industrious; when the rule that they
who do not work shall not eat will be applied not to
paupers only, but impartially to all; when the division
of the produce of labour, instead of depending, as in so
great a degree it now does, on the accident of birth, will
be made by concert on an acknowledged principle of
justice; and when it will no longer either be, or be thought
to be, impossible for human beings to exert themselves
strenuously in procuring benefits which are not to be
exclusively their own, but to be shared with the society
they belong to. The social problem of the future we considered to be, how to unite the greatest individual liberty
of action with a common ownership in the raw material
of the globe, and an equal participation of all in the
benefits of combined labour. We had not the presumption
to suppose that we could already foresee by what precise form of institutions these objects could most effectually
be attained, or at how near or how distant a period they
would become practicable. We saw clearly that to render
any such social transformation either possible or desirable, an equivalent change of character must take place
both in the uncultivated herd who now compose the
labouring masses, and in the immense majority of their
employers. Both these classes must learn by practice to
labour and combine for generous, or at all events for
public and social purposes, and not, as hitherto, solely for
narrowly interested ones. But the capacity to do this
has always existed in mankind, and is not, nor is ever
likely to be, extinct. Education, habit, and the cultivation
of the sentiments will make a common man dig or weave
for his country, as readily as fight for his country. True
enough, it is only by slow degrees, and a system of culture prolonged through successive generations, that men
in general can be brought up to this point. But the hindrance is not in the essential constitution of human nature.
Interest in the common good is at present so weak a
motive in the generality, not because it can never be
otherwise, but because the mind is not accustomed to
dwell on it as it dwells from morning till night on things

which tend only to personal advantage. When called into activity, as only self-interest now is, by the daily course of life, and spurred from behind by the love of distinction and the fear of shame, it is capable of producing, even in common men, the most strenuous exertions as well as the most heroic sacrifices. The deep-rooted selfishness which forms the general character of the existing state of society, is *so* deeply rooted, only because the whole course of existing institutions tends to foster it; and modern institutions in some respects more than ancient, since the occasion on which the individual is called on to do anything for the public without receiving its pay are far less frequent in modern life than in the smaller commonwealths of antiquity. These considerations did not make us overlook the folly of premature attempts to dispense with the inducements of private interest in social affairs, while no substitute for them has been or can be provided; but we regarded all existing institutions and social arrangements as being (in a phrase I once heard from Austin) "merely provisional," and we welcomed with the greatest pleasure and interest all socialistic experiments by select individuals (such as the Co-operative Societies), which, whether they succeeded or failed, could not but operate as a most useful education of those who took part in them, by cultivating their capacity of acting upon motives pointing directly to the general good, or making them aware of the defects which render them and others incapable of doing so.

In the *Principles of Political Economy*, these opinions were promulgated, less clearly and fully in the first edition, rather more so in the second, and quite unequivocally in the third. The difference arose partly from the change of times, the first edition having been written and sent to press before the French Revolution of 1848, after which the public mind became more open to the reception of novelties in opinion, and doctrines appeared moderate which would have been thought very startling a short time before. In the first edition the difficulties of socialism were stated so strongly that the tone was on the whole that of opposition to it. In the year of two which followed, much time was given to the study of the best socialistic writers on the Continent, and to meditation and discussion on the whole range of topics in-

volved in the controversy; and the result was that most of
what had been written on the subject in the first edition
was cancelled, and replaced by arguments and reflections
which represent a more advanced opinion.

The *Political Economy* was far more rapidly executed
than the *Logic,* or indeed than anything of importance
which I had previously written. It was commenced in the
autumn of 1845, and was ready for the press before the
end of 1847. In this period of little more than two years
there was an interval of six months during which the work
was laid aside, while I was writing articles in the *Morning
Chronicle* (which unexpectedly entered warmly into my
purpose), urging the formation of peasant properties on
the waste lands of Ireland. This was during the period of
the Famine, the winter of 1846-47, when the stern necessities of the time seemed to afford a chance of gaining
attention for what appeared to me the only mode of
combining relief to immediate destitution with permanent
improvement of the social and economical condition of
the Irish people. But the idea was new and strange; there
was no English precedent for such a proceeding; and the
profound ignorance of English politicians and the English
public concerning all social phenomena not generally met
with in England (however common elsewhere), made my
endeavours an entire failure. Instead of a great operation
on the waste lands, and the conversion of cottiers into
proprietors, Parliament passed a Poor Law for maintaining them as paupers; and if the nation has not since found
itself in inextricable difficulties from the joint operation
of the old evils and the quack remedy, it is indebted for its
deliverance to that most unexpected and surprising fact,
the depopulation of Ireland, commenced by famine, and
continued by emigration.

The rapid success of the *Political Economy* showed
that the public wanted, and were prepared for such
a book. Published early in 1848, an edition of a thou-
sand copies was sold in less than a year. Another similar
edition was published in the spring of 1849; and a third,
of 1,250 copies, early in 1852. It was, from the first,
continually cited and referred to as an authority, because
it was not a book merely of abstract science, but also
of application, and treated political economy not as a
thing by itself, but as a fragment of a greater whole; a

branch of social philosophy so interlinked with all the other branches that its conclusions, even in its own peculiar province, are only true conditionally, subject to interference and counteraction from causes not directly within its scope—while to the character of a practical guide it has no pretension, apart from other classes of considerations. Political economy, in truth, has never pretended to give advice to mankind with no lights but its own; though people who knew nothing but political economy (and therefore knew that ill) have taken upon themselves to advise, and could only do so by such lights as they had. But the numerous sentimental enemies of political economy, and its still more numerous interested enemies in sentimental guise, have been very successful in gaining belief for this among other unmerited imputations against it, and the *Principles* having, in spite of the freedom of many of its opinions, become for the present the most popular treatise on the subject, has helped to disarm the the enemies of so important a study. The amount of its worth as an exposition of the science, and the value of the different applications which it suggests, others of course must judge.

For a considerable time after this, I published no work of magnitude; though I still occasionally wrote in periodicals, and my correspondence (much of it with persons quite unknown to me), on subjects of public interest, swelled to a considerable bulk. During these years I wrote or commenced various essays, for eventual publication, on some of the fundamental questions of human and social life, with regard to several of which I have already much exceeded the severity of the Horatian precept. I continued to watch with keen interest the progress of public events. But it was not, on the whole, very encouraging to me. The European reaction after 1848, and the success of an unprincipled usurper in December, 1851, put an end, as it seemed, to all present hope of freedom or social improvement in France and the Continent. In England, I had seen and continued to see many of the opinions of my youth obtain general recognition, and many of the reforms in institutions, for which I had through life contended, either effected or in course of being so. But these changes had been attended with much less benefit to human well-being than

I should formerly have anticipated, because they had produced very little improvement in that which all real amelioration in the lot of mankind depends on, their intellectual and moral state; and it might even be questioned if the various causes of deterioration which had been at work in the meanwhile, had not more than counterbalanced the tendencies to improvement. I had learnt from experience that many false opinions may be exchanged for true ones, without in the least altering the habits of mind of which false opinions are the result. The English public, for example, are quite as raw and undiscerning on subjects of political economy since the nation has been converted to free trade as they were before; and are still further from having acquired better habits of thought or feeling, or being in any way better fortified against error, on subjects of a more elevated character. For, though they have thrown off certain errors, the general discipline of their minds, intellectually and morally, is not altered. I am now convinced that no great improvements in the lot of mankind are possible until a great change takes place in the fundamental constitution of their modes of thought. The old opinions in religion, morals, and politics are so much discredited in the more intellectual minds as to have lost the greater part of their efficacy for good, while they have still life enough in them to be a powerful obstacle to the growing up of any better opinions on those subjects. When the philosophic minds of the world can no longer believe its religion, or can only believe it with modifications amounting to an essential change of its character, a transitional period commences, of weak convictions, paralysed intellects, and growing laxity of principle, which cannot terminate until a renovation has been effected in the basis of their belief, leading to the evolution of some faith, whether religious or merely human, which they can really believe; and when things are in this state, all thinking or writing which does not tend to promote such a renovation is of very little value beyond the moment. Since there was little in the apparent condition of the public mind indicative of any tendency in this direction, my view of the immediate prospects of human improvement was not sanguine. More recently a spirit of free speculation has sprung up, giving a more encouraging prospect of the gradual mental emancipation of England; and concurring with the renewal, under better auspices, of the movement for political freedom in the rest of Europe, has given to the present condition of human affairs a more hopeful aspect.*

Between the time of which I have now spoken, and the present, took place the most important events of my private life. The first of these was my marriage, in April, 1851, to the lady whose incomparable worth had made her friendship the greatest source to me both of happiness and of improvement during many years in which we never expected to be in any closer relation to one another. Ardently as I should have aspired to this complete union of our lives at any time in the course of my existence at which it had been practicable, I, as much as my wife, would far rather have foregone that privilege forever than have owed it to the premature death of one for whom I had the sincerest respect, and she the strongest affection. That event, however, having taken place in July, 1849, it was granted to me to derive from that evil my own greatest good, by adding to the partnership of thought, feeling, and writing which had long existed, a partnership of our entire existence. For seven and a half years that blessing was mine; for seven and a half only! I can say nothing which could describe, even in the faintest manner, what that loss was and is. But because I know that she would have wished it, I endeavour to make the best of what life I have left, and to work on for her purposes with such diminished strength as can be derived from thoughts of her, and communion with her memory.

When two persons have their thoughts and speculations completely in common; when all subjects of intellectual or moral interest are discussed between them in daily life, and probed to much greater depths than are usually or conveniently sounded in writings intended for general readers; when they set out from the same principles, and arrive at their conclusions by processes pursued jointly, it is of little consequence, in respect to the question of originality, which of them holds the pen; the one who contributes least to the composition may contribute most to the thought; the writings which result are the

* Written about 1861.

joint product of both, and it must often be impossible to disentangle their respective parts, and affirm that this belongs to one and that to the other. In this wide sense, not only during the years of our married life, but during many of the years of confidential friendship which preceded, all my published writings were as much her work as mine; her share in them constantly increasing as years advanced. But in certain cases, what belongs to her can be distinguished, and specially identified. Over and above the general influence which her mind had over mine, the most valuable ideas and features in these joint productions—those which have been most fruitful of important results, and have contributed most to the success and reputation of the works themselves—originated with her, were emanations from her mind, my part in them being no greater than in any of the thoughts which I found in previous writers, and made my own only by incorporating them with my own system of thought. During the greater part of my literary life I have performed the office in relation to her, which from a rather early period I had considered as the most useful part that I was qualified to take in the domain of thought: that of an interpreter of original thinkers, and mediator between them and the public; for I had always a humble opinion of my own powers as an original thinker, except in abstract science (logic, metaphysics, and the theoretic principles of political economy and politics), but thought myself much superior to most of my contemporaries in willingness and ability to learn from everybody; as I found hardly any one who made such a point of examining what was said in defence of all opinions, however new or however old, in the conviction that even if they were errors there might be a substratum of truth underneath them, and that in any case the discovery of what it was that made them plausible would be a benefit to truth. I had, in consequence, marked this out as a sphere of usefulness in which I was under a special obligation to make myself active; the more so as the acquaintance I had formed with the ideas of the Coleridgians, of the German thinkers, and of Carlyle, all of them fiercely opposed to the mode of thought in which I had been brought up, had convinced me that along with much error they possessed much truth, which was veiled from minds otherwise capable of receiving it by the transcendental and mystical phraseology in which they were accustomed to shut it up, and from which they neither cared, nor knew how, to disengage it; and I did not despair of separating the truth from the error, and exposing it in terms which would be intelligible and not repulsive to those on my own side in philosophy. Thus prepared, it will easily be believed that when I came into close intellectual communion with a person of the most eminent faculties, whose genius, as it grew and unfolded itself in thought, continually struck out truths far in advance of me, but in which I could not, as I had done in those others, detect any mixture of error, the greatest part of my mental growth consisted in the assimilation of those truths, and the most valuable part of my intellectual work was in building the bridges and clearing the paths which connected them with my general system of thought.*

* The steps in my mental growth for which I was indebted to her were far from being those which a person wholly uninformed on the subject would probably suspect. It might be supposed, for instance, that my strong convictions on the complete equality in all legal, political, social and domestic relations, which ought to exist between men and women, may have been adopted or learnt from her. This was so far from being the fact that those convictions were among the earliest results of the application of my mind to political subjects, and the strength with which I held them was, as I believe, more than anything else, the originating cause of the interest she felt in me. What is true is that until I knew her, the opinion was, in my mind, little more than an abstract principle. I saw no more reason why women should be held in legal subjection to other people than why men should. I was certain that their interests required fully as much protection as those of men, and were quite as little likely to obtain it without an equal voice in making the laws by which they were to be bound. But that perception of the vast practical bearings of women's disabilities which found expression in the book on the *Subjection of Women* was acquired mainly through her teaching. But for her rare knowledge of human nature and comprehension of moral and social influences, though I should doubtless have held my present opinions, I should have had a very insufficient perception of the mode in which the consequences of the inferior position of women intertwine themselves with all the evils of existing society and with all the difficulties of human improvement. I am indeed painfully conscious of how much of her best thoughts on the subject I have failed to reproduce, and how greatly that little treatise falls short of what would have been if she had put on paper her entire mind on this question, or had lived to revise and improve, as

The first of my books in which her share was conspicuous was the *Principles of Political Economy*. The *System of Logic* owed little to her except in the minuter matters of composition, in which respect my writings, both great and small, have largely benefited by her accurate and clear-sighted criticism.* The chapter of the *Political Economy* which has had a greater influence on opinion than all the rest, that on "the Probable Future of the Labouring Classes," is entirely due to her; in the first draft of the book, that chapter did not exist. She pointed out the need of such a chapter, and the extreme imperfection of the book without it; she was the cause of my writing it; and the more general part of the chapter, the statement and discussion of the two opposite theories respecting the proper condition of the labouring classes, was wholly an exposition of her thoughts, often in words taken from her own lips. The purely scientific part of the *Political Economy* I did not learn from her; but it was chiefly her influence that gave to the book that general tone by which it is distinguished from all previous expositions of political economy that had any pretension to being scientific, and which has made it so useful in conciliating minds which those previous expositions had

---

she certainly would have done, my imperfect statement of the case.

* The only person from whom I received any direct assistance in the preparation of the *System of Logic* was Mr. Bain, since so justly celebrated for his philosophical writings. He went carefully through the manuscript before it was sent to press, and enriched it with a great number of additional examples and illustrations from science; many of which, as well as some detached remarks of his own in confirmation of my logical views, I inserted nearly in his own words.

My obligations to Comte were only to his writings—to the part which had then been published of his *Système de Philosophie Positive* and, as has been seen from what I have already said in this narrative, the amount of these obligations is far less than has sometimes been asserted. The first volume, which contains all the fundamental doctrines of the book, was substantially complete before I had seen Comte's treatise. I derived from him many valuable thoughts, conspicuously in the chapter on "Hypotheses" and in the view taken of the logic of algebra; but it is only in the concluding Book, on the "Logic of the Moral Sciences," that I owe to him any radical improvement in my conception of the application of logical method. This improvement I have stated and characterized in a former part of the present memoir.

repelled. This tone consisted chiefly in making the proper
distinction between the laws of the production of wealth,
which are real laws of nature, dependent on the properties of objects, and the modes of its distribution, which,
subject to certain conditions, depend on human will. The
common run of political economists confuse these together, under the designation of economic laws, which
they deem incapable of being defeated or modified by
human effort; ascribing the same necessity to things dependent on the unchangeable conditions of our earthly
existence, and to those which, being but the necessary
consequences of particular social arrangements, are merely
coextensive with these: given certain institutions and
customs, wages, profits, and rent will be determined by
certain causes; but this class of political economists drop
the indispensable presupposition, and argue that these
causes must, by an inherent necessity, against which no
human means can avail, determine the shares which fall,
in the division of the produce, to labourers, capitalists,
and landlords. The *Principles of Political Economy* yielded
to none of its predecessors in aiming at the scientific appreciation of the action of these causes, under the conditions which they presuppose; but it set the example
of not treating those conditions as final. The economic
generalizations which depend not on necessities of nature
but on those combined with the existing arrangements of
society it deals with only as provisional, and as liable
to be much altered by the progress of social improvement.
I had indeed partially learnt this view of things from the
thoughts awakened in me by the speculations of the
Saint-Simonians; but it was made a living principle pervading and animating the book by my wife's promptings.
This example illustrates well the general character of what
she contributed to my writings. What was abstract and
purely scientific was generally mine; the properly human
element came from her: in all that concerned the application of philosophy to the exigencies of human society
and progress, I was her pupil, alike in boldness of speculation and cautiousness of practical judgement. For, on
the one hand, she was much more courageous and far-
sighted than without her I should have been, in anticipations of an order of things to come, in which many of
the limited generalizations now so often confounded with

universal principles will cease to be applicable. Those parts of my writings, and especially of the *Political Economy*, which contemplate possibilities in the future such as, when affirmed by socialists, have in general been fiercely denied by political economists, would, but for her, either have been absent, or the suggestions would have been made much more timidly and in a more qualified form. But while she thus rendered me bolder in speculation on human affairs, her practical turn of mind, and her almost unerring estimate of practical obstacles, repressed in me all tendencies that were really visionary. Her mind invested all ideas in a concrete shape, and formed to itself a conception of how they would actually work, and her knowledge of the existing feelings and conduct of mankind was so seldom at fault that the weak point in any unworkable suggestion seldom escaped her.*

During the years which intervened between the commencement of my married life and the catastrophe which closed it, the principal occurrences of my outward existence (unless I count as such a first attack of the family disease, and a consequent journey of more than six months for the recovery of health, in Italy, Sicily, and Greece), had reference to my position in the India House. In 1856 I was promoted to the rank of chief of the office in which I had served for upwards of thirty-three years. The appointment, that of Examiner of India Correspondence, was the highest, next to that of Secretary, in the East India Company's home service, involving the general superintendence of all the correspondence with the Indian Governments, except the military, naval, and financial. I held this office as long as it continued to exist, being a little more than two years; after which it pleased Parliament, in other words Lord Palmerston, to put an end to the East India Company as a branch of the Government of India under the Crown, and convert the administration of that country into a thing to be scrambled for by the second and third class of English parliamentary politicians. I was the chief manager of the resistance which the Company made to their own political

* A few dedicatory lines acknowledging what the book owed to her were prefixed to some of the presentation copies of the *Political Economy* on its first publication. Her dislike of publicity alone prevented their insertion in the other copies of the work.

extinction, and to the letters and petitions I wrote for them, and the concluding chapter of my treatise on *Representative Government*, I must refer for my opinions on the folly and mischief of this ill-considered change. Personally I considered myself a gainer by it, as I had given enough of my life to India, and was not unwilling to retire on the liberal compensation granted. After the change was consummated, Lord Stanley, the First Secretary of State for India, made me the honourable offer of a seat in the Council, and the proposal was subsequently renewed by the Council itself, on the first occasion of its having to supply a vacancy in its own body. But the conditions of Indian Government under the new system made me anticipate nothing but useless vexation and waste of effort from any participation in it; and nothing that has since happened has had any tendency to make me regret my refusal.

During the two years which immediately preceded the cessation of my official life, my wife and I were working together at the *Liberty*. I had first planned and written it as a short essay in 1854. It was in mounting the steps of the Capitol, in January, 1855, that the thought first arose of converting it into a volume. None of my writings have been either so carefully composed, or so sedulously corrected as this. After it had been written as usual twice over, we kept it by us, bringing it out from time to time, and going through it *de novo*, reading, weighing, and criticizing every sentence. Its final revision was to have been a work of the winter of 1858-59, the first after my retirement, which we had arranged to pass in the South of Europe. That hope and every other were frustrated by the most unexpected and bitter calamity of her death—at Avignon, on our way to Montpellier, from a sudden attack of pulmonary congestion.

Since then I have sought for such alleviation as my state admitted of, by the mode of life which most enabled me to feel her still near me. I bought a cottage as close as possible to the place where she is buried, and there her daughter (my fellow sufferer and now my chief comfort), and I live constantly during a great portion of the year. My objects in life are solely those which were hers; my pursuits and occupations those in which she shared, or sympathized, and which are indissolubly associated with her. Her memory is to me a religion, and her approbation the standard, by which, summing up as it does all worthiness, I endeavour to regulate my life.*

After my irreparable loss, one of my earliest cares was to print and publish the treatise, so much of which was the work of her whom I had lost, and consecrate it to her memory. I have made no alteration or addition to it, nor shall I ever. Though it wants the last touch of her hand, no substitute for that touch shall ever be attempted by mine.

The *Liberty* was more directly and literally our joint production than anything else which bears my name, for there was not a sentence of it which was not several times gone through by us together, turned over in many ways, and carefully weeded of any faults, either in thought or expression, that we detected in it. It is in consequence of this that although it never underwent her final revision, it far surpasses, as a mere specimen of composition, anything which has proceeded from me either before or since. With regard to the thoughts, it is difficult to identify any particular part or element as being more hers than all the rest. The whole mode of thinking, of which the book was the expression, was emphatically hers. But I also was so thoroughly imbued with it that the same thoughts naturally occurred to us both. That I was thus penetrated with it, however, I owe in a great degree to her. There was a moment in my mental progress when I might easily have fallen into a tendency towards over-government, both social and political; as there was also a moment when, by reaction from a contrary excess, I might have become a less thorough Radical and Democrat than I am. In both these points, as in many others, she benefited me as much by keeping me right where I was right as by leading me to new truths, and ridding me of errors. My great readiness and eagerness to learn from everybody, and to make room in my opinions for every new acquisition by adjusting the old and the new to one another, might, but for her steadying influence, have seduced me into modifying my early opinions too much. She was in nothing more valuable to my mental develop-

* What precedes was written or revised previous to, or during the year 1861. What follows was written in 1870.

ment than by her just measure of the relative importance of different considerations, which often protected me from allowing to truths I had only recently learnt to see a more important place in my thoughts than was properly their due.

The *Liberty* is likely to survive longer than anything else that I have written (with the possible exception of the *Logic*), because the conjunction of her mind with mine has rendered it a kind of philosophic text-book of a single truth, which the changes progressively taking place in modern society tend to bring out into ever stronger relief: the importance, to man and society, of a large variety in types of character, and of giving full freedom to human nature to expand itself in innumerable and conflicting directions. Nothing can better show how deep are the foundations of this truth, than the great impression made by the exposition of it at a time which, to superficial observation, did not seem to stand much in need of such a lesson. The fears we expressed, lest the inevitable growth of social equality and of the government of public opinion should impose on mankind an oppressive yoke of uniformity in opinion and practice, might easily have appeared chimerical to those who looked more at present facts than at tendencies; for the gradual revolution that is taking place in society and institutions has, thus far, been decidedly favourable to the development of new opinions, and has procured for them a much more unprejudiced hearing than they previously met with. But this is a feature belonging to periods of transition, when old notions and feelings have been unsettled, and no new doctrines have yet succeeded to their ascendancy. At such times people of any mental activity, having given up their old beliefs, and not feeling quite sure that those they still retain can stand unmodified, listen eagerly to new opinions. But this state of things is necessarily transitory: some particular body of doctrine in time rallies the majority round it, organizes social institutions and modes of action conformably to itself; education impresses this new creed upon the new generations without the mental processes that have led to it, and by degrees it acquires the very same power of compression so long exercised by the creeds of which it had taken the place. Whether this noxious power will be exercised depends on whether mankind have by that time become aware that it cannot be exercised without stunting and dwarfing human nature. It is then that the teachings of the *Liberty* will have their greatest value. And it is to be feared that they will retain that value a long time.

As regards originality, it has of course no other than that which every thoughtful mind gives to its own mode of conceiving and expressing truths which are common property. The leading thought of the book is one which, though in many ages confined to insulated thinkers, mankind have probably at no time since the beginning of civilization been entirely without. To speak only of the last few generations, it is distinctly contained in the vein of important thought respecting education and culture spread through the European mind by the labours and genius of Pestalozzi. The unqualified championship of it by Wilhelm von Humboldt is referred to in the book; but he by no means stood alone in his own country. During the early part of the present century the doctrine of the rights of individuality, and the claim of the moral nature to develop itself in its own way, was pushed by a whole school of German authors even to exaggeration; and the writings of Goethe, the most celebrated of all German authors, though not belonging to that or to any other school, are penetrated throughout by views of morals and of conduct in life often in my opinion not defensible, but which are incessantly seeking whatever defence they admit of in the theory of the right and duty of self-development. In our own country, before the book *On Liberty* was written, the doctrine of individuality had been enthusiastically asserted, in a style of vigorous declamation sometimes reminding one of Fichte, by Mr. William Maccall in a series of writings of which the most elaborate is entitled *Elements of Individualism,* and a remarkable American, Mr. Warren, had formed a system of society, on the foundation of the "sovereignty of the individual," had obtained a number of followers, and had actually commenced the formation of a village community (whether it now exists I know not), which, though bearing a superficial resemblance to some of the projects of socialists, is diametrically opposite to them in principle, since it recognizes no authority whatever in society over the individual, except to enforce equal freedom of development for all individualities. As the book which bears my name claimed no originality for any of its doctrines, and was not intended to write their history, the only author who had preceded me in their assertion, of whom I thought it appropriate to say anything, was Humboldt, who furnished the motto to the work; although in one passage I borrowed from the Warrenites their phrase, the sovereignty of the individual. It is hardly necessary here to remark that there are abundant differences in detail between the conception of the doctrine by any of the predecessors I have mentioned and that set forth in the book.

The political circumstances of the time induced me, shortly after, to complete and publish a pamphlet (*Thoughts on Parliamentary Reform*), part of which had been written some years previously, on the occasion of one of the abortive Reform Bills, and had at the time been approved and revised by her. Its principal features were, hostility to the ballot (a change of opinion in both of us, in which she rather preceded me), and a claim of representation for minorities; not, however, at that time going beyond the cumulative vote proposed by Mr. Garth Marshall. In finishing the pamphlet for publication, with a view to the discussions on the Reform Bill of Lord Derby's and Mr. Disraeli's government in 1859, I added a third feature, a plurality of votes, to be given, not to property, but to proved superiority of education. This recommended itself to me as a means of reconciling the irresistible claim of every man or woman to be consulted, and to be allowed a voice, in the regulation of affairs which vitally concern them, with the superiority of weight justly due to opinions grounded on superiority of knowledge. The suggestion, however, was one which I had never discussed with my almost infallible counsellor, and I have no evidence that she would have concurred in it. As far as I have been able to observe, it has found favour with nobody; all who desire any sort of inequality in the electoral vote, desiring it in favour of property and not of intelligence or knowledge. If it ever overcomes the strong feeling which exists against it, this will only be after the establishment of a systematic national education by which the various grades of politically valuable acquirement may be accurately defined and authenticated. Without this it will always remain liable to strong, possibly conclusive, objections; and with this, it would perhaps not be needed.

It was soon after the publication of *Thoughts on Parliamentary Reform* that I became acquainted with Mr. Hare's admirable system of personal representation, which, in its present shape, was then for the first time publshed. I saw in this great practical and philosophical idea the greatest improvement of which the system of representative government is susceptible; an improvement which, in the most felicitous manner, exactly meets and cures the grand, and what before seemed the inherent, defect of the representative system; that of giving to a numerical majority all power, instead of only a power proportional to its numbers, and enabling the strongest party to exclude all weaker parties from making their opinions heard in the assembly of the nation, except through such opportunity as may be given to them by the accidentally unequal distribution of opinions in different localities. To these great evils nothing more than very imperfect palliations had seemed possible; but Mr. Hare's system affords a radical cure. This great discovery, for it is no less, in the political art, inspired me, as I believe it has inspired all thoughtful persons who have adopted it, with new and more sanguine hopes respecting the prospects of human society; by freeing the form of political institutions towards which the whole civilized world is manifestly and irresistibly tending from the chief part of what seemed to qualify, or render doubtful, its ultimate benefits. Minorities, so long as they remain minorities, are, and ought to be, outvoted; but under arrangements which enable any assemblage of voters, amounting to a certain number, to place in the legislature a representative of its own choice, minorities cannot be suppressed. Independent opinions will force their way into the council of the nation and make themselves heard there, a thing which often cannot happen in the existing forms of representative democracy; and the legislature, instead of being weeded of individual peculiarities and entirely made up of men who simply represent the creed of great political or religious parties, will comprise a large portion of the most eminent individual minds in the country, placed there, without reference to party, by voters who appreciate their individual eminence. I can understand that persons, otherwise intelligent, should, for want of suf-

ficient examination, be repelled from Mr. Hare's plan by
what they think the complex nature of its machinery. But
any one who does not feel the want which the scheme is
intended to supply; any one who throws it over as a mere
theoretical subtlety or crotchet, tending to no valuable purpose, and unworthy of the attention of practical men, may
be pronounced an incompetent statesman, unequal to the
politics of the future. I mean, unless he is a minister or
aspires to become one; for we are quite accustomed to a
minister continuing to profess unqualified hostility to an
improvement almost to the very day when his conscience,
or his interest, induces him to take it up as a public measure, and carry it.

Had I met with Mr. Hare's system before the publication of my pamphlet, I should have given an account of
it there. Not having done so, I wrote an article in *Fraser's
Magazine* (reprinted in my miscellaneous writings) principally for that purpose, though I included in it,
along with Mr. Hare's book, a review of two other productions on the question of the day; one of them a pamphlet
by my early friend, Mr. John Austin, who had in his old
age become an enemy to all further parliamentary reform;
the other an able and vigorous, though partially erroneous
work by Mr. Lorimer.

In the course of the same summer I fulfilled a duty
particularly incumbent upon me, that of helping (by an
article in the *Edinburgh Review*) to make known Mr.
Bain's profound treatise on the *Mind*, just then completed
by the publication of its second volume. And I carried
through the press a selection of my minor writings, forming the first two volumes of *Dissertations and Discussions*.
The selection had been made during my wife's lifetime,
but the revision, in concert with her, with a view to re-
publication, had been barely commenced; and when I
had no longer the guidance of her judgement I despaired
of pursuing it further, and republished the papers as they
were, with the exception of striking out such passages
as were no longer in accordance with my opinions. My
literary work of the year was terminated with an essay
in *Fraser's Magazine* (afterwards republished in the third
volume of *Dissertations and Discussions*), entitled "A Few
Words on Non-intervention." I was prompted to write this
paper by a desire, while vindicating England from the

imputations commonly brought against her on the Continent of a peculiar selfishness in matters of foreign policy, to warn Englishmen of the colour given to this imputation by the low tone in which English statesmen are accustomed to speak of English policy as concerned only with English interests, and by the conduct of Lord Palmerston at that particular time in opposing the Suez Canal; and I took the opportunity of expressing ideas which had long been in my mind (some of them generated by my Indian experience, and others by the international questions which then greatly occupied the European public), respecting the true principles of international morality, and the legitimate modifications made in it by difference of times and circumstances; a subject I had already, to some extent, discussed in the vindication of the French Provisional Government of 1848 against the attacks of Lord Brougham and others, which I published at the time in the *Westminster Review,* and which is reprinted in the *Dissertations.*

I had now settled, as I believed, for the remainder of my existence into a purely literary life; if that can be called literary which continued to be occupied in a pre-eminent degree with politics, and not merely with theoretical, but practical politics, although a great part of the year was spent at a distance of many hundred miles from the chief seat of the politics of my own country, to which, and primarily for which, I wrote. But, in truth, the modern facilities of communication have not only removed all the disadvantages, to a political writer in tolerably easy circumstances, of distance from the scene of political action, but have converted them into advantages. The immediate and regular receipt of newspapers and periodicals keeps him *au courant* of even the most temporary politics, and gives him a much more correct view of the state and progress of opinion than he could acquire by personal contact with individuals: for every one's social intercourse is more or less limited to particular sets or classes, whose impressions and no others reach him through that channel; and experience has taught me that those who give their time to the absorbing claims of what is called society, not having leisure to keep up a large acquaintance with the organs of opinion, remain much more ignorant of the general state either of the public mind, or of the active and instructed part of it, than a recluse who reads the newspapers need be. There are, no doubt, disadvantages in too long a separation from one's country—in not occasionally renewing one's impressions of the light in which men and things appear when seen from a position in the midst of them; but the deliberate judgement formed at a distance, and undisturbed by inequalities of perspective, is the most to be depended on, even for application to practice. Alternating between the two positions, I combined the advantages of both. And, though the inspirer of my best thoughts was no longer with me, I was not alone; she had left a daughter, my stepdaughter   *   *   *   *   *

*   *   whose ever growing and ripening talents from that day to this have been devoted to the same great purposes.   *   *   *

*   *   *   *   *

Surely no one ever before was so fortunate as, after such a loss as mine, to draw another prize in the lottery of life.   *   *   *   *   *

*   *   Whoever, either now or hereafter, may I think of me of the work I have done, must never forget that it is the product not of one intellect and conscience, but of three.   *   *   *

*   *   *   *   *   *

*   *   *   *   *   *   *

The work of the years 1860 and 1861 consisted chiefly of two treatises, only one of which was intended for immediate publication. This was the *Considerations on Representative Government*; a connected exposition of what, by the thoughts of many years, I had come to regard as the best form of a popular constitution. Along with as much of the general theory of government as is necessary to support this particular portion of its practice, the volume contains my matured views of the principal questions which occupy the present age, within the province of purely organic institutions, and raises, by anticipation, some other questions to which growing necessities will sooner or later compel the attention both of theoretical and of practical politicians. The chief of these last is the distinction between the function of making laws, for which a numerous popular assembly is radically unfit,

and that of getting good laws made, which is its proper
duty and cannot be satisfactorily fulfilled by any other
authority; and the consequent need of a legislative commission as a permanent part of the constitution of a free
country, consisting of a small number of highly trained
political minds, on whom, when Parliament has determined that a law shall be made, the task of making it
should be devolved; Parliament retaining the power of
passing or rejecting the bill when drawn up, but not of altering it otherwise than by sending proposed amendments
to be dealt with by the commission. The question here
raised respecting the most important of all public functions,
that of legislation, is a particular case of the great problem
of modern political organization, stated, I believe, for the
first time in its full extent by Bentham, though in my opinion not always satisfactorily resolved by him; the combination of complete popular control over public affairs,
with the greatest attainable perfection of skilled agency.

The other treatise written at this time is the one which
was published some years later* under the title of *The
Subjection of Women*. It was written   *   *
*   *   that there might, in any event,
be in existence a written exposition of my opinions on
that great question, as full and conclusive as I could
make it. The intention was to keep this among other
unpublished papers, improving it from time to time if I
was able, and to publish it at the time when it should seem
likely to be most useful. As ultimately published in what
was of my own composition, all that is most striking and
profound belongs to my wife, coming from the fund of
thought which had been made common to us both, by
our innumerable conversations and discussions on a topic
which filled so large a place in our minds.

Soon after this time I took from their repository a portion of the unpublished papers which I had written during
the last years of our married life, and shaped them, with
some additional matter, into the little work entitled *Utilitarianism;* which was first published, in three parts, in
successive numbers of *Fraser's Magazine,* and afterwards
reprinted in a volume.

Before this, however, the state of public affairs had
become extremely critical, by the commencement of the

* In 1869.

American Civil War. My strongest feelings were engaged in this struggle, which, I felt from the beginning, was destined to be a turning point, for good or evil, of the course of human affairs for an indefinite duration. Having been a deeply interested observer of the slavery quarrel in America, during the many years that preceded the open breach, I knew that it was in all its stages an aggressive enterprise of the slave owners to extend the territory of slavery under the combined influences of pecuniary interest, domineering temper, and the fanaticism of a class for its class privileges, influences so fully and powerfully depicted in the admirable work of my friend Professor Cairnes, *The Slave Power*. Their success, if they succeeded, would be a victory of the powers of evil which would give courage to the enemies of progress and damp the spirits of its friends all over the civilized world, while it would create a formidable military power, grounded on the worst and most antisocial form of the tyranny of men over men, and, by destroying for a long time the prestige of the great democratic republic, would give to all the privileged classes of Europe a false confidence, probably to be extinguished in blood. On the other hand, if the spirit of the North was sufficiently roused to carry the war to a successful termination, and if that termination did not come too soon and too easily, I foresaw, from the laws of human nature, and the experience of revolutions, that when it did come it would in all probability be thorough: that the bulk of the Northern population, whose conscience had as yet been awakened only to the point of resisting the further extension of slavery, but whose fidelity to the Constitution of the United States made them disapprove of any attempt by the Federal Government to interfere with slavery in the states where it already existed, would acquire feelings of another kind when the Constitution had been shaken off by armed rebellion, would determine to have done for ever with the accursed thing, and would join their banner with that of the noble body of Abolitionists, of whom Garrison was the courageous and single-minded apostle, Wendell Phillips the eloquent orator, and John Brown the voluntary martyr.*

* The saying of this true hero, after his capture, that he was worth more for hanging than for any other purpose, reminds one, by its combination of wit, wisdom, and self-devotion, of Sir Thomas More.

Then, too, the whole mind of the United States would be let loose from its bonds, no longer corrupted by the supposed necessity of apologizing to foreigners for the most flagrant of all possible violations of the free principles of their Constitution; while the tendency of a fixed state of society to stereotype a set of national opinions would be at least temporarily checked, and the national mind would become more open to the recognition of whatever was bad in either the institutions or the customs of the people. These hopes, so far as related to slavery, have been completely, and in other respects are in course of being progressively realized. Foreseeing from the first this double set of consequences from the success or failure of the rebellion, it may be imagined with what feelings I contemplated the rush of nearly the whole upper and middle classes of my own country, even those who passed for Liberals, into a furious pro-Southern partisanship; the working classes and some of the literary and scientific men, being almost the sole exceptions to the general frenzy. I never before felt so keenly how little permanent improvement had reached the minds of our influential classes, and of what small value were the Liberal opinions they had got into the habit of professing. None of the Continental Liberals committed the same frightful mistake. But the generation which had extorted Negro emancipation from our West India planters had passed away; another had succeeded which had not learnt by many years of discussion and exposure to feel strongly the enormities of slavery; and the inattention habitual with Englishmen to whatever is going on in the world outside their own island made them profoundly ignorant of all the antecedents of the struggle, insomuch that it was not generally believed in England, for the first year or two of the war, that the quarrel was one of slavery. There were men of high principle and unquestionable liberality of opinion who thought it a dispute about tariffs, or assimilated it to the cases, in which they were accustomed to sympathize, of a people struggling for independence.

It was my obvious duty to be one of the small minority who protested against this perverted state of public opinion. I was not the first to protest. It ought to be remembered to the honour of Mr. Hughes and of Mr. Ludlow that they, by writings published at the very beginning of the struggle, began the protestation. Mr. Bright followed in one of the most powerful of his speeches, followed by others not less striking. I was on the point of adding my word to theirs, when there occurred, towards the end of 1861, the seizure of the Southern envoys on board a British vessel, by an officer of the United States. Even English forgetfulness has not yet had time to lose all re-membrance of the explosion of feeling in England which then burst forth, the expectation, which prevailed for some weeks, of war with the United States, and the warlike preparations actually commenced on this side. While this state of things lasted, there was no chance of a hearing for anything favourable to the American cause; and, more-over, I agreed with those who thought the act unjustifiable, and such as to require that England should demand its dis-avowal. When the disavowal came, and the alarm of war was over, I wrote, in January, 1862, the paper, in *Fra-ser's Magazine*, entitled "The Contest in America."   *   *   *   * Written and published when it was, this paper helped to encourage those Liberals who had felt overborne by the tide of illiberal opinion, and to form in favour of the good cause a nucleus of opinion which increased gradually, and, after the success of the North began to seem probable, rapidly. When we returned from our journey I wrote a second article, a review of Professor Cairnes' book, published in the *Westminster Review*. England is paying the penalty, in many uncomfort-able ways, of the durable resentment which her ruling classes stirred up in the United States by their ostentatious wishes for the ruin of America as a nation; they have reason to be thankful that a few, if only a few, known writers and speakers, standing firmly by the Americans in the time of their greatest difficulty, effected a partial di-version of these bitter feelings, and made Great Britain not altogether odious to the Americans.

This duty having been performed, my principal occupa-tion for the next two years was on subjects not political. The publication of Mr. Austin's *Lectures on Jurisprudence*, after his decease, gave me an opportunity of paying a de-served tribute to his memory, and at the same time ex-pressing some thoughts on a subject on which, in my old days of Benthamism, I had bestowed much study. But the chief product of those years was the *Examination of Sir*

William Hamilton's Philosophy. His Lectures, published in 1860 and 1861, I had read towards the end of the latter year, with a half-formed intention of giving an account of them in a review, but I soon found that this would be idle, and that justice could not be done to the subject in less than a volume. I had then to consider whether it would be advisable that I myself should attempt such a performance. On consideration, there seemed to be strong reasons for doing so. I was greatly disappointed with the *Lectures*. I read them, certainly, with no prejudice against Sir William Hamilton. I had up to that time deferred the study of his notes to *Reid* on account of their unfinished state, but I had not neglected his *Discussions on Philosophy*; and though I knew that his general mode of treating the facts of mental philosophy differed from that of which I most approved, yet his vigorous polemic against the later Transcendentalists, and his strenuous assertion of some important principles, especially the relativity of human knowledge, gave me many points of sympathy with his opinions, and made me think that genuine psychology had considerably more to gain than to lose by his authority and reputation. His *Lectures* and the dissertations on *Reid* dispelled this illusion; and even the *Discussions,* read by the light which these throw on them, lose much of their value. I found that the points of apparent agreement between his opinions and mine were more verbal than real; that the important philosophical principles which I had thought he recognized were so explained away by him as to mean little or nothing, or were continually lost sight of, and doctrines entirely inconsistent with them were taught in nearly every part of his philosophical writings. My estimation of him was therefore so far altered that instead of regarding him as occupying a kind of intermediate position between the two rival philosophies, holding some of the principles of both, and supplying to both powerful weapons of attack and defence, I now looked upon him as one of the pillars, and in this country from his high philosophical reputation the chief pillar, of that one of the two which seemed to me to be erroneous.

Now, the difference between these two schools of philosophy, that of intuition, and that of experience and association, is not a mere matter of abstract speculation; it is full of practical consequences, and lies at the foundation of all the greatest differences of practical opinion in an age of progress. The practical reformer has continually to demand that changes be made in things which are supported by powerful and widely spread feelings, or to question the apparent necessity and indefeasibleness of established facts; and it is often an indispensable part of his argument to show, how those powerful feelings had their origin, and how those facts came to seem necessary and indefeasible. There is therefore a natural hostility between him and a philosophy which discourages the explanation of feelings and moral facts by circumstances and association, and prefers to treat them as ultimate elements of human nature; a philosophy which is addicted to holding up favourite doctrines as intuitive truths, and deems intuition to be the voice of Nature and of God, speaking with an authority higher than that of our reason. In particular, I have long felt that the prevailing tendency to regard all the marked distinctions of human character as innate, and in the main indelible, and to ignore the irresistible proofs that by far the greater part of those differences, whether between individuals, races, or sexes, are such as not only might but naturally would be produced by differences in circumstances, is one of the chief hindrances to the rational treatment of great social questions, and one of the greatest stumbling blocks to human improvement. This tendency has its source in the intuitional metaphysics which characterized the reaction of the nineteenth century against the eighteenth, and it is a tendency so agreeable to human indolence, as well as to conservative interests generally, that unless attacked at the very root, it is sure to be carried to even a greater length than is really justified by the more moderate forms of the intuitional philosophy. That philosophy, not always in its moderate forms, had ruled the thought of Europe for the greater part of a century. My father's *Analysis of the Mind*, my own *Logic*, and professor Bain's great treatise, had attempted to reintroduce a better mode of philosophizing, latterly with quite as much success as could be expected; but I had for some time felt that the mere contrast of the two philosophies was not enough, that there ought to be a hand-to-hand fight between them, that controversial as well as expository writings were needed, and that the time was come when such controversy would be useful. Considering then the writings and fame of Sir W. Hamilton as the great fortress of the intuitional philosophy in this country, a fortress the more formidable from the imposing character, and the in-many-respects great personal merits and mental endowments, of the man, I thought it might be a real service to philosophy to attempt a thorough examination of all his most important doctrines, and an estimate of his general claims to eminence as a philosopher, and I was confirmed in this resolution by observing that in the writings of at least one, and him one of the ablest, of Sir W. Hamilton's followers, his peculiar doctrines were made the justification of a view of religion which I hold to be profoundly immoral—that it is our duty to bow down in worship before a Being whose moral attributes are affirmed to be unknowable by us, and to be perhaps extremely different from those which, when we are speaking of our fellow creatures, we call by the same names.

As I advanced in my task, the damage to Sir W. Hamilton's reputation became greater than I at first expected, through the almost incredible multitude of inconsistencies which showed themselves on comparing different passages with one another. It was my business, however, to show things exactly as they were, and I did not flinch from it. I endeavoured always to treat the philosopher whom I criticized with the most scrupulous fairness; and I knew that he had abundance of disciples and admirers to correct me if I ever unintentionally did him injustice. Many of them accordingly have answered me, more or less elaborately; and they have pointed out oversights and misunderstandings, though few in number, and mostly very unimportant in substance. Such of those as had (to my knowledge) been pointed out before the publication of the latest edition (at present the third) have been corrected there, and the remainder of the criticisms have been, as far as seemed necessary, replied to. On the whole, the book has done its work: it has shown the weak side of Sir William Hamilton, and has reduced his too great philosophical reputation within more moderate bounds; and by some of its discussions, as well as by two expository chapters, on the notions of matter and of mind, it has perhaps thrown additional light on some of the disputed questions in the domain of psychology and metaphysics.

After the completion of the book on Hamilton, I applied myself to a task which a variety of reasons seemed to render specially incumbent upon me; that of giving an account, and forming an estimate, of the doctrines of Auguste Comte. I had contributed more than any one else to make his speculations known in England, and, in consequence chiefly of what I had said of him in my *Logic,* he had readers and admirers among thoughtful men on this side of the Channel at a time when his name had not yet in France emerged from obscurity. So unknown and unappreciated was he at the time when my *Logic* was written and published that to criticize his weak points might well appear superfluous, while it was a duty to give as much publicity as one could to the important contributions he had made to philosophic thought. At the time, however, at which I have now arrived, this state of affairs had entirely changed. His name, at least, was known almost universally, and the general character of his doctrines very widely. He had taken his place, in the estimation of both friends and opponents, as one of the conspicuous figures in the thought of the age. The better parts of his speculations had made great progress in working their way into those minds, which, by their previous culture and tendencies, were fitted to receive them; under cover of those better parts those of a worse character, greatly developed and added to in his later writings, had also made some way, having obtained active and enthusiastic adherents, some of them of no inconsiderable personal merit, in England, France, and other countries. These causes not only made it desirable that some one should undertake the task of sifting what is good from what is bad in M. Comte's speculations, but seemed to impose on myself in particular a special obligation to make the attempt. This I accordingly did in two essays, published in successive numbers of the *Westminster Review,* and reprinted in a small volume under the title *Auguste Comte and Positivism.*

The writings which I have not mentioned, together with a small number of papers in periodicals which I have not deemed worth preserving, were the whole of the products of my activity as a writer during the years from 1859 to 1865. In the early part of the last-mentioned year, in compliance with a wish frequently expressed to me by

working men, I published cheap People's Editions of
those of my writings which seemed the most likely to
find readers among the working classes; viz., *Principles
of Political Economy, Liberty, and Representative Government*. This was a considerable sacrifice of my pecuniary interest, especially as I resigned all idea of deriving
profit from the cheap editions, and after ascertaining from
my publishers the lowest price which they thought would
remunerate them on the usual terms of an equal division
of profits, I gave up my half share to enable the price
to be fixed still lower. To the credit of Messrs. Longman
they fixed, unasked, a certain number of years after
which the copyright and stereotype plates were to re-
vert to me, and a certain number of copies after the
sale of which I should receive half of any further profit.
This number of copies (which in the case of the *Political
Economy* was 10,000) has for some time been exceeded,
and the People's Editions have begun to yield me a small
but unexpected pecuniary return, though very far from
an equivalent for the diminution of profit from the Library Editions.

In this summary of my outward life I have now arrived
at the period at which my tranquil and retired existence
as a writer of books was to be exchanged for the less
congenial occupation of a member of the House of Commons. The proposal made to me early in 1865, by some
electors of Westminster, did not present the idea to me
for the first time. It was not even the first offer I had received, for, more than ten years previous, in consequence
of my opinions on the Irish Land question, Mr. Lucas
and Mr. Duffy, in the name of the popular party in Ireland, offered to bring me into Parliament for an Irish
county, which they could easily have done; but the in-
compatibility of a seat in Parliament with the office I
then held in the India House precluded even consideration of the proposal. After I had quitted the India House,
several of my friends would gladly have seen me a member of Parliament; but there seemed no probability that
the idea would ever take any practical shape. I was convinced that no numerous or influential portion of any
electoral body really wished to be represented by a person of my opinions; and that one who possessed no local
connexion or popularity, and who did not choose to stand

as the mere organ of a party, had small chance of being elected anywhere unless through the expenditure of money. Now it was, and is, my fixed conviction, that a candidate ought not to incur one farthing of expense for undertaking a public duty. Such of the lawful expenses of an election as have no special reference to any particular candidate ought to be borne as a public charge, either by the State or by the locality. What has to be done by the supporters of each candidate in order to bring his claims properly before the constituency should be done by unpaid agency, or by voluntary subscription. If members of the electoral body, or others, are willing to subscribe money of their own for the purpose of bringing, by lawful means, into Parliament someone who they think would be useful there, no one is entitled to object; but that the expense, or any part of it, should fall on the candidate is fundamentally wrong; because it amounts in reality to buying his seat. Even on the most favourable supposition as to the mode in which the money is expended, there is a legitimate suspicion that any one who gives money for leave to undertake a public trust has other than public ends to promote by it; and (a consideration of the greatest importance) the cost of elections, when borne by the candidates, deprives the nation of the services, as members of Parliament, of all who cannot or will not afford to incur a heavy expense. I do not say that so long as there is scarcely a chance for an independent candidate to come into Parliament without complying with this vicious practice, it must always be morally wrong in him to spend money, provided that no part of it is either directly or indirectly employed in corruption. But, to justify it, he ought to be very certain that he can be of more use to his country as a member of Parliament than in any other mode which is open to him; and this assurance, in my own case, I did not feel. It was by no means clear to me that I could do more to advance the public objects which had a claim on my exertions from the benches of the House of Commons than from the simple position of a writer. I felt, therefore, that I ought not to seek election to Parliament, much less to expend any money in procuring it.

But the conditions of the question were considerably altered when a body of electors sought me out, and spontaneously offered to bring me forward as their candidate. If it should appear, on explanation, that they persisted in this wish, knowing my opinions, and accepting the only conditions on which I could conscientiously serve, it was questionable whether this was not one of those calls upon a member of the community by his fellow citizens which he was scarcely justified in rejecting. I therefore put their disposition to the proof by one of the frankest explanations ever tendered, I should think, to an electoral body by a candidate. I wrote, in reply to the offer, a letter for publication, saying that I had no personal wish to be a member of Parliament, that I thought a candidate ought neither to canvass nor to incur any expense, and that I could not consent to do either. I said further that if elected, I could not undertake to give any of my time and labour to their local interests. With respect to general politics, I told them without reserve, what I thought on a number of important subjects on which they had asked my opinion; and one of these being the suffrage, I made known to them, among other things, my conviction (as I was bound to do, since I intended, if elected, to act on it), that women were entitled to representation in Parliament on the same terms with men. It was the first time doubtless, that such a doctrine had ever been mentioned to English electors; and the fact that I was elected after proposing it gave the start to the movement, which has since become so vigorous, in favour of women's suffrage. Nothing, at the time, appeared more unlikely than that a candidate (if candidate I could be called) whose professions and conduct set so completely at defiance all ordinary notions of electioneering should nevertheless be elected. A well-known literary man was heard to say that the Almighty himself would have no chance of being elected on such a programme. I strictly adhered to it, neither spending money nor canvassing, nor did I take any personal part in the election, until about a week preceding the day of nomination, when I attended a few public meetings to state my principles and give answers to any questions which the electors might exercise their just right of putting to me for their own guidance; answers as plain and unreserved as my address. On one subject only, my religious opinions, I announced from the beginning that I would answer no questions; a determination which appeared to be completely approved by those who attended the meetings. My frankness on all other subjects on which I was interrogated evidently did me far more good than my answers, whatever they might be, did harm. Among the proofs I received of this, one is too remarkable not to be recorded. In the pamphlet, *Thoughts on Parliamentary Reform,* I had said, rather bluntly, that the working classes, though differing from those of some other countries in being ashamed of lying, are yet generally liars. This passage some opponent got printed in a placard, which was handed to me at a meeting, chiefly composed of the working classes, and I was asked whether I had written and published it. I at once answered, "I did." Scarcely were these two words out of my mouth, when vehement applause resounded through the whole meeting. It was evident that the working people were so accustomed to expect equivocation and evasion from those who sought their suffrages that when they found, instead of that, a direct avowal of what was likely to be disagreeable to them, instead of being affronted, they concluded at once that this was a person whom they could trust. A more striking instance never came under my notice of what, I believe, is the experience of those who best know the working classes, that the most essential of all recommendations to their favour is that of complete straightforwardness; its presence outweighs in their minds very strong objections, while no amount of other qualities will make amends for its apparent absence. The first working-man who spoke after the incident I have mentioned (it was Mr. Odger), said that the working classes had no desire not to be told of their faults; they wanted friends, not flatterers, and felt under obligation to any one who told them anything in themselves which he sincerely believed to require amendment. And to this the meeting heartily responded.

Had I been defeated in the election, I should still have had no reason to regret the contact it had brought me into with large bodies of my countrymen; which not only gave me much new experience, but enabled me to scatter my political opinions more widely, and, by making me known in many quarters where I had never before been heard of, increased the number of my readers, and the presumable influence of my writings. These latter effects were of course produced in a still greater degree, when, as much to my surprise as to that of any one, I was returned to Parliament by a majority of some hundreds over my Conservative competitor.

I was a member of the House during the three sessions of the Parliament which passed the Reform Bill; during which time Parliament was necessarily my main occupation, except during the recess. I was a tolerably frequent speaker, sometimes of prepared speeches, sometimes extemporaneously. But my choice of occasions was not such as I should have made if my leading object had been parliamentary influence. When I had gained the ear of the House, which I did by a successful speech on Mr. Gladstone's Reform Bill, the idea I proceeded on was that when anything was likely to be as well done, or sufficiently well done, by other people, there was no necessity for me to meddle with it. As I, therefore, in general reserved myself for work which no others were likely to do, a great proportion of my appearances were on points on which the bulk of the Liberal party, even the advanced portion of it, either were of a different opinion from mine, or were comparatively indifferent. Several of my speeches, especially one against the motion for the abolition of capital punishment, and another in favour of resuming the right of seizing enemies' goods in neutral vessels, were opposed to what then was, and probably still is, regarded as the advanced Liberal opinion. My advocacy of women's suffrage and of personal representation were at the time looked upon by many as whims of my own; but the great progress since made by those opinions, and especially the response made from almost all parts of the kingdom to the demand for women's suffrage, fully justified the timeliness of those movements, and have made what was undertaken as a moral and social duty, a personal success. Another duty which was particularly incumbent on me, as one of the metropolitan members, was the attempt to obtain a municipal government for the metropolis; but on that subject the indifference of the House of Commons was such that I found hardly any help or support within its walls. On this subject, however, I was the organ of an active and intelligent body of persons outside, with whom, and not with me, the scheme originated, and drew up the bills. My part was to bring in bills already prepared, and to sustain the discussion of them during the short time they were allowed to remain before the House; after having taken an active part in the work of a committee presided over by Mr. Ayrton, which sat through the greater part of the session of 1866, to take evidence on the subject. The very different position in which the question now stands (1870) may justly be attributed to the preparation which went on during those years, and which produced but little visible effect at the time; but all questions on which there are strong private interests on one side, and only the public good on the other, have a similar period of incubation to go through.

The same idea, that the use of my being in Parliament was to do work which others were not able or not willing to do, made me think it my duty to come to the front in defence of advanced Liberalism on occasions when the obloquy to be encountered was such as most of the advanced Liberals in the House preferred not to incur. My first vote in the House was in support of an amendment in favour of Ireland, moved by an Irish member, and for which only five English and Scotch votes were given, including my own; the other four were Mr. Bright, Mr. McLaren, Mr. T. B. Potter, and Mr. Hadfield. And the second speech I delivered* was on the Bill to prolong the suspension of the habeas corpus in Ireland. In denouncing, on this occasion, the English mode of governing Ireland, I did no more than the general opinion of England now admits to have been just; but the anger against Fenianism was then in all its freshness; any attack on what Fenians attacked was looked upon as an apology for them; and I was so unfavourably received by the House that more than one of my friends advised me (and my own judgment agreed with the advice), to wait, before speaking again, for the favourable opportunity that would be given by the first great debate on the Reform Bill. During this silence, many flattered themselves that I had turned out a failure, and that they should not be troubled with me any more.

* The first was in answer to Mr. Lowe's reply to Mr. Bright on the Cattle Plague Bill, and was thought at the time to have helped to get rid of a provision in the Government measure which would have given to landholders a second indemnity after they had already been once indemnified for the loss of some of their cattle by the increased selling price of the remainder.

Perhaps their uncomplimentary comments may, by the force of reaction, have helped to make my speech on the Reform Bill the success it was. My position in the House was further improved by a speech in which I insisted on the duty of paying off the national debt before our coal supplies are exhausted, and by an ironical reply to some of the Tory leaders who had quoted against me certain passages of my writings, and called me to account for others, especially for one in my *Considerations on Representative Government,* which said that the Conservative party was, by the law of its composition, the stupidest party. They gained nothing by drawing attention to the passage, which up to that time had not excited any notice, but the sobriquet of "the stupid party" stuck to them for a considerable time afterwards. Having now no longer any apprehension of not being listened to, I confined myself, as I have since thought too much, to occasions on which my services seemed specially needed, and abstained more than enough from speaking on the great party questions. With the exception of Irish questions, and those which concerned the working classes, a single speech on Mr. Disraeli's Reform Bill was nearly all that I contributed to the great decisive debates of the last two of my three sessions.

I have, however, much satisfaction in looking back to the part I took on the two classes of subjects just mentioned. With regard to the working classes, the chief topic of my speech on Mr. Gladstone's Reform Bill was the assertion of their claims to the suffrage. A little later, after the resignation of Lord Russell's Ministry and the succession of a Tory Government, came the attempt of the working classes to hold a meeting in Hyde Park, their exclusion by the police, and the breaking down of the park railing by the crowd. Though Mr. Beales and the leaders of the the working-men had retired under protest when this took place, a scuffle ensued in which many innocent persons were maltreated by the police, and the exasperation of the working-men was extreme. They showed a determination to make another attempt at a meeting in the Park, to which many of them would probably have come armed; the Government made military preparations to resist the attempt, and something very serious seemed impending. At this crisis I really believe that I was the means of preventing much mischief. I had in my place in Parliament taken the side of the working-men, and strongly censured the conduct of the Government. I was invited, with several other Radical members, to a conference with the leading members of the Council of the Reform League; and the task fell chiefly upon myself, of persuading them to give up the Hyde Park project, and hold their meeting elsewhere. It was not Mr. Beales and Colonel Dickson who needed persuading; on the contrary, it was evident that these gentlemen had already exerted their influence in the same direction, thus far without success. It was the working-men who held out, and so bent were they on their original scheme that I was obliged to have recourse to *les grands moyens*. I told them that a proceeding which would certainly produce a collision with the military could only be justifiable on two conditions: if the position of affairs had become such that a revolution was desirable, and if they thought themselves able to accomplish one. To this argument, after considerable discussion, they at last yielded; and I was able to inform Mr. Walpole that their intention was given up. I shall never forget the depth of his relief or the warmth of his expressions of gratitude. After the working-men had conceded so much to me, I felt bound to comply with their request that I would attend and speak at their meeting at the Agricultural Hall, the only meeting called by the Reform League which I ever attended. I had always declined being a member of the League, on the avowed ground that I did not agree in its programme of manhood suffrage and the ballot: from the ballot I dissented entirely; and I could not consent to hoist the flag of manhood suffrage, even on the assurance that the exclusion of women was not intended to be implied; since if one goes beyond what can be immediately carried, and professes to take one's stand on a principle, one should go the whole length of the principle. I have entered thus particularly into this matter because my conduct on this occasion gave great displeasure to the Tory and Tory-Liberal press, who have charged me ever since with having shown myself, in the trials of public life, intemperate and passionate. I do not know what they expected from me; but they had reason to be thankful to me if they knew from what I had, in all probability, preserved them. And I do not believe it could have been done, at that particular juncture, by any one else. No other person, I believe, had at that moment the necessary influence for restraining the working classes, except Mr. Gladstone and Mr. Bright, neither of whom was available: Mr. Gladstone for obvious reasons; Mr. Bright because he was out of town.

When, some time later, the Tory Government brought in a Bill to prevent public meetings in the Parks, I not only spoke strongly in opposition to it, but formed one of a number of advanced Liberals, who, aided by the very late period of the session, succeeded in defeating the Bill by what is called talking it out. It has not since been renewed.

On Irish affairs also I felt bound to take a decided part. I was one of the foremost in the deputation of members of Parliament who prevailed on Lord Derby to spare the life of the condemned Fenian insurgent, General Burke. The Church question was so vigorously handled by the leaders of the party, in the session of 1868, as to require no more from me than an emphatic adhesion; but the land question was by no means in so advanced a position: the superstitions of landlordism had up to that time been little challenged, especially in Parliament, and the backward state of the question, so far as concerned the parliamentary mind, was evidenced by the extremely mild measure brought in by Lord Russell's Government in 1866, which nevertheless could not be carried. On that Bill I delivered one of my most careful speeches, in which I attempted to lay down some of the principles of the subject, in a manner calculated less to stimulate friends, than to conciliate and convince opponents. The engrossing subject of parliamentary reform prevented either this Bill, or one of a similar character brought in by Lord Derby's Government, from being carried through. They never got beyond the second reading. Meanwhile the signs of Irish disaffection had become much more decided; the demand for complete separation between the two countries had assumed a menacing aspect, and there were few who did not feel that if there was still any chance of reconciling Ireland to the British connexion, it could only be by the adoption of much more thorough reforms in the territorial and social relations of the country than had yet been contemplated. The time seemed to me to have come when it would be useful to speak out my whole mind;

and the result was my pamphlet *England and Ireland,* which was written in the winter of 1867, and published shortly before the commencement of the session of 1868. The leading features of the pamphlet were, on the one hand, an argument to show the undesirableness, for Ireland as well as for England, of separation between the countries, and on the other, a proposal for settling the land question by giving to the existing tenants a permanent tenure, at a fixed rent, to be assessed after due inquiry by the State.

The pamphlet was not popular, except in Ireland, as I did not expect it to be. But if no measure short of that which I proposed would do full justice to Ireland, or afford a prospect of conciliating the mass of the Irish people, the duty of proposing it was imperative; while if, on the other hand, there was any intermediate course which had a claim to a trial, I well knew that to propose something which would be called extreme was the true way not to impede but to facilitate a more moderate experiment. It is most improbable that a measure conceding so much to the tenantry as Mr. Gladstone's Irish Land Bill, would have been proposed by a Government, or could have been carried through Parliament, unless the British public had been led to perceive that a case might be made, and perhaps a party formed, for a measure considerably stronger. It is the character of the British people, or at least of the higher and middle classes who pass muster for the British people, that to induce them to approve of any change, it is necessary that they should look upon it as a middle course: they think every proposal extreme and violent unless they hear of some other proposal going still farther, upon which their antipathy to extreme views may discharge itself. So it proved in the present instance; my proposal was condemned, but any scheme for Irish Land reform, short of mine, came to be thought moderate by comparison. I may observe that the attacks made on my plan usually gave a very incorrect idea of its nature. It was usually discussed as a proposal that the State should buy up the land and become the universal landlord; though in fact it only offered to each individual landlord this as an alternative, if he liked better to sell his estate than to retain it on the new conditions; and I fully anticipated that most landlords would continue to prefer the position of landowners to that of Government annuitants, and would retain their existing relation to their tenants, often on more indulgent terms than the full rents on which the compensation to be given them by Government would have been based. This and many other explanations I gave in a speech on Ireland, in the debate on Mr. Maguire's resolution, early in the session of 1868. A corrected report of this speech, together with my speech on Mr. Fortescue's Bill, has been published (not by me, but with my permission) in Ireland.

Another public duty, of a most serious kind, it was my lot to have to perform, both in and out of Parliament, during these years. A disturbance in Jamaica, provoked in the first instance by injustice, and exaggerated by rage and panic into a premediated rebellion, had been the motive or excuse for taking hundreds of innocent lives by military violence, or by sentence of what were called courts martial, continuing for weeks after the brief disturbance had been put down; with many added atrocities of destruction of property, flogging women as well as men, and a general display of the brutal recklessness which usually prevails when fire and sword are let loose. The perpetrators of those deeds were defended and applauded in England by the same kind of people who had so long upheld Negro slavery; and it seemed at first as if the British nation was about to incur the disgrace of letting pass, without even a protest, excesses of authority as revolting as any of those for which, when perpetrated by the instruments of other governments, Englishmen can hardly find terms sufficient to express their abhorrence. After a short time, however, an indignant feeling was roused; a voluntary association formed itself under the name of the Jamaica Committee to take such deliberation and action as the case might admit of, and adhesions poured in from all parts of the country. I was abroad at the time, but I sent in my name to the Committee as soon as I heard of it, and took an active part in the proceedings from the time of my return. There was much more at stake than only justice to the Negroes, imperative as was that consideration. The question was, whether the British dependencies, and eventually, perhaps, Great Britain itself, were to be under the government of law, or of military licence; whether the lives and persons of

British subjects are at the mercy of any two or three officers, however raw and inexperienced or reckless and brutal, whom a panic-stricken Governor, or other functionary, may assume the right to constitute into a so-called court martial. This question could only be decided by an appeal to the tribunals; and such an appeal the Committee determined to make. Their determination led to a change in the chairmanship of the Committee, as the chairman, Mr. Charles Buxton, thought it not unjust indeed, but inexpedient, to prosecute Governor Eyre and his principal subordinates in a criminal court; but a numerously attended general meeting of the Association having decided this point against him, Mr. Buxton withdrew from the Committee, though continuing to work in the cause, and I was, quite unexpectedly on my own part, proposed and elected chairman. It became, in consequence, my duty to represent the Committee in the House of Commons, sometimes by putting questions to the Government, sometimes as the recipient of questions, more or less provocative, addressed by individual members to myself; but especially as speaker in the important debate originated in the session of 1866 by Mr. Buxton; and the speech I then delivered is that which I should probably select as the best of my speeches in Parliament.* For more than two years we carried on the combat, trying every avenue legally open to us, to the Courts of Criminal Justice. A bench of magistrates in one of the most Tory counties in England dismissed our case; we were more successful before the magistrates at Bow Street; which gave an opportunity to the Lord Chief Justice of the Queen's Bench Sir Alexander Cockburn, for delivering his celebrated charge, which settled the law of the question in favour of liberty, as far as it is in the power of a judge's charge to settle it. There, however, our success ended, for the Old Bailey Grand Jury by throwing out our Bill prevented the case from coming to trial. It was clear that to bring English functionaries to the bar of a criminal court for abuses of power committed against Negroes

---

* Among the most active members of the Committee were Mr. P.A. Taylor, M.P., always faithful and energetic in every assertion of the principles of liberty; Mr. Goldwin Smith, Mr. Frederick Harrison, Mr. Slack, Mr. Chamerovzow, Mr. Shaen, and Mr. Chesson, the Honorary Secretary of the Association.

and mulattoes was not a popular proceeding with the English middle classes. We had, however, redeemed, so far as lay in us, the character of our country, by showing that there was at any rate a body of persons determined to use all the means which the law afforded to obtain justice for the injured. We had elicited from the highest criminal judge in the nation an authoritative declaration that the law was what we maintained it to be; and we had given an emphatic warning to those who might be tempted to similar guilt hereafter that, though they might escape the actual sentence of a criminal tribunal, they were not safe against being put to some trouble and expense in order to avoid it. Colonial governors and other persons in authority will have a considerable motive to stop short of such extremities in future.

As a matter of curiosity I kept some specimens of the abusive letters, almost all of them anonymous, which I received while these proceedings were going on. They are evidence of the sympathy felt with the brutalities in Jamaica by the brutal part of the population at home. They graduated from coarse jokes, verbal and pictorial, up to threats of assassination.

Among other matters of importance in which I took an active part, but which excited little interest in the public, two deserve particular mention. I joined with several other independent Liberals in defeating an Extradition Bill introduced at the very end of the session of 1866, and by which, though surrender avowedly for political offences was not authorized, political refugees, if charged by a foreign Government with acts which are necessarily incident to all attempts at insurrection, would have been surrendered to be dealt with by the criminal courts of the Government against which they had rebelled thus making the British Government an accomplice in the vengeance of foreign despotisms. The defeat of this proposal led to the appointment of a Select Committee (in which I was included), to examine and report on the whole subject of extradition treaties; and the result was that in the Extradition Act which passed through Parliament after I had ceased to be a member, opportunity is given to any one whose extradition is demanded, of being heard before an English court of justice to prove that the offence with which he is charged is really political. The cause of

European freedom has thus been saved from a great iniquity. The other subject to be mentioned is the fight kept up by a body of advanced Liberals in the session of 1868, on the Bribery Bill of Mr. Disraeli's Government, in which I took a very active part. I had taken counsel with several of those who had applied their minds most carefully to the details of the subject—Mr. W. D. Christie, Serjeant Pulling, Mr. Chadwick—as well as bestowed much thought of my own, for the purpose of framing such amendments and additional clauses as might make the Bill really effective against the numerous modes of corruption, direct and indirect, which might otherwise, as there was much reason to fear, be increased instead of diminished by the Reform Act. We also aimed at en-grafting on the Bill measures for diminishing the mis-chievous burden of what are called the legitimate expenses of elections. Among our many amendments was that of Mr. Fawcett for making the returning officer's expenses a charge on the rates, instead of on the candidates; an-other was the prohibition of paid canvassers, and the limitation of paid agents to one for each candidate; a third was the extension of the precautions and penalties against bribery, to municipal elections, which are well known to be not only a preparatory school for bribery at parliamentary elections, but an habitual cover for it. The Conservative Government, however, when once they had carried the leading provision of their Bill (for which I voted and spoke), the transfer of the jurisdiction in elections from the House of Commons to the judges, made a determined resistance to all other improvements; and after one of the most important proposals, that of Mr. Fawcett, had actually obtained a majority, they summoned the strength of their party and threw out the clause in a subsequent stage. The Liberal party in the House was greatly dishonoured by the conduct of many of its mem-bers in giving no help whatever to this attempt to secure the necessary conditions of an honest representation of the people. With their large majority in the House they could have carried all the amendments, or better ones if they had better to propose. But it was late in the session; members were eager to set about their preparations for the impending general election; and while some (such as Sir Robert Anstruther) honourably remained at their

post, though rival candidates were already canvassing
their constituency, a much greater number placed their
electioneering interests before their public duty. Many
Liberals also looked with indifference on legislation
against bribery, thinking that it merely diverted public
interest from the ballot, which they considered, very mis-
takenly as I expect it will turn out, to be a sufficient, and
the only, remedy. From these causes our fight, though
kept up with great vigour for several nights, was wholly
unsuccessful, and the practices which we sought to render more difficult prevailed more widely than ever in the
first general election held under the new electoral law.

In the general debates on Mr. Disraeli's Reform Bill,
my participation was limited to the one speech already
mentioned; but I made the Bill an occasion for bringing
the two greatest improvements which remain to be made
in representative government formally before the House
and the nation. One of them was personal, or, as it is
called with equal propriety, proportional representation.
I brought this under the consideration of the House by
an expository and argumentative speech on Mr. Hare's
plan; and subsequently I was active in support of the
very imperfect substitute for that plan, which, in a small
number of constituencies, Parliament was induced to
adopt. This poor makeshift had scarcely any recommendation, except that it was a partial recognition of the evil
which it did so little to remedy. As such, however, it
was attacked by the same fallacies, and required to be
defended on the same principles as a really good measure; and its adoption in a few parliamentary elections, as
well as the subsequent introduction of what is called the
cumulative vote in the elections for the London
School Board, have had the good effect of converting
the equal claim of all electors to a proportional share
in the representation from a subject of merely speculative discussion into a question of practical politics, much
sooner than would otherwise have been the case.

This assertion of my opinions on personal representation cannot be credited with any considerable or visible amount of practical result. It was otherwise with
the other motion which I made in the form of an amendment to the Reform Bill, and which was by far the
most important, perhaps the only really important, pub-

lic service I performed in the capacity of a member of
Parliament: a motion to strike out the words which were
understood to limit the electoral franchise to males, and
thereby to admit to the suffrage all women who, as house-
holders or otherwise, possessed the qualification required
of male electors. For women not to make their claim
to the suffrage, at the time when the elective franchise
was being largely extended, would have been to abjure
the claim altogether; and a movement on the subject was
begun in 1866, when I presented a petition for the suffrage, signed by a considerable number of distinguished
women. But it was as yet uncertain whether the proposal would obtain more than a few stray votes in the
House; and when, after a debate in which the speakers on
the contrary side were conspicuous by their feebleness,
the votes recorded in favour of the motion amounted
to 73—made up by pairs and tellers to above 80—the
surprise was general, and the encouragement great: the
greater, too, because one of those who voted for the motion was Mr. Bright, a fact which could only be attributed to the impression made on him by the debate, as he
had previously made no secret of his non-concurrence in
the proposal.   *   *   *   *   *   *
I believe I have mentioned all that is worth remembering of my proceedings in the House. But their enumera-
tion, even if complete, would give but an inadequate idea
of my occupations during that period, and especially of the
time taken up by correspondence. For many years before
my election to Parliament, I had been continually receiving letters from strangers, mostly addressed to me as a
writer on philosophy, and either propounding difficulties
or communicating thoughts on subjects connected with
logic or political economy. In common, I suppose, with all
who are known as political economists, I was a recipient
of all the shallow theories and absurd proposals by which
people are perpetually endeavouring to show the way to
universal wealth and happiness by some artful reorganiza-
tion of the currency. When there were signs of sufficient
intelligence in the writers to make it worth-while attempting to put them right, I took the trouble to point out their
errors, until the growth of my correspondence made it
necessary to dismiss such persons with very brief answers.
Many, however, of the communications I received were

more worthy of attention than these, and in some, over-sights of detail were pointed out in my writings, which I was thus enabled to correct. Correspondence of this sort naturally multiplied with the multiplication of the subjects on which I wrote, especially those of a metaphysical character. But when I became a member of Parliament, I began to receive letters on private grievances and on every imaginable subject that related to any kind of public affairs, however remote from my knowledge or pursuits. It was not my constituents in Westminster who laid this burden on me: they kept with remarkable fidelity to the understanding on which I had consented to serve. I received, indeed, now and then an application from some ingenuous youth to procure for him a small Government appointment; but these were few, and how simple and ignorant the writers were was shown by the fact that the applications came in about equally whichever party was in power. My invariable answer was that it was contrary to the principles on which I was elected to ask favours of any Government. But, on the whole, hardly any part of the country gave me less trouble than my own constituents. The general mass of correspondence, however, swelled into an oppressive burden.   *   *   *   *

     *   *   *   *   *   *

*   *   *   *   *   *   *

     *   *   *   *   *   *

While I remained in Parliament my work as an author was unavoidably limited to the recess. During that time I wrote (besides the pamphlet on Ireland, already mentioned), the "Essay on Plato," published in the *Edinburgh Review*, and reprinted in the third volume of *Dissertations and Discussions*; and the address which, conformably to custom, I delivered to the University of St. Andrew's, whose students had done me the honour of electing me to the office of Rector. In this discourse I gave expression to many thoughts and opinions which had been accumulating in me through life, respecting the various studies which belong to a liberal education, their uses and influences, and the mode in which they should be pursued to render their influences most beneficial. The position taken up, vindicating the high educational value alike of the old classic and the new scientific studies, on even stronger grounds than are urged by most of their advocates, and insisting that it is only the stupid inefficiency of the usual teaching which makes those studies be regarded as competitors instead of allies, was, I think, calculated not only to aid and stimulate the improvement which has happily commenced in the national institutions for higher education, but to diffuse juster ideas than we often find, even in highly educated men, on the conditions of the highest mental cultivation.

During this period also I commenced (and completed soon after I had left Parliament) the performance of a duty to philosophy and to the memory of my father, by preparing and publishing an edition of the *Analysis of the Phenomena of the Human Mind,* with notes bringing up the doctrines of that admirable book to the latest improvements in science and in speculation. This was a joint undertaking, the psychological notes being furnished in about equal proportions by Mr. Bain and myself, while Mr. Grote supplied some valuable contributions on points in the history of philosophy incidentally raised, and Dr. Andrew Findlater supplied the deficiencies in the book which had been occasioned by the imperfect philological knowledge of the time when it was written. Having been originally published at a time when the current of metaphysical speculation ran in a quite opposite direction to the psychology of experience and association, the *Analysis* had not obtained the amount of immediate success which it deserved, though it had made a deep impression on many individual minds, and had largely contributed, through those minds, to create that more favourable atmosphere for the association psychology of which we now have the benefit. Admirably adapted for a class-book of the experience metaphysics, it only required to be enriched, and in some cases corrected, by the results of more recent labours in the same school of thought, to stand, as it now does, in company with Mr. Bain's treatises, at the head of the systematic works on analytic psychology.

In the autumn of 1868 the Parliament which passed the Reform Act was dissolved, and at the new election for Westminister I was thrown out; not to my surprise, nor, I believe, to that of my principal supporters, though in the few days preceding the election they had become more sanguine than before. That I should not have been elected at all would not have required any explanation; what excites curiosity is that I should have been elected the first time, or, having been elected then, should have been defeated afterwards. But the efforts made to defeat me were far greater on the second occasion than on the first. For one thing, the Tory Government was now struggling for existence, and success in any contest was of more importance to them. Then, too, all persons of Tory feelings were far more embittered against me individually than on the previous occasion; many who had at first been either favourable or indifferent were vehemently opposed to my re-election. As I had shown in my political writings that I was aware of the weak points in democratic opinions, some Conservatives, it seems, had not been without hopes of finding me an opponent of democracy; as I was able to see the Conservative side of the question, they presumed that, like them I could not see any other side. Yet if they had really read my writings, they would have known that after giving full weight to all that appeared to me well grounded in the arguments against democracy, I unhesitatingly decided in its favour, while recommending that it should be accompanied by such institutions as were consistent with its principle calculated to ward off its inconveniences: one of the chief of these remedies being proportional Representation, on which scarcely any of the Conservatives gave me any support. Some Tory expectations appear to have been founded on the approbation I had expressed of plural voting, under certain conditions; and it has been surmised that the suggestion of this sort made in one of the resolutions which Mr. Disraeli introduced into the House preparatory to his Reform Bill (a suggestion which meeting with no favour he did not press), may have been occasioned by what I had written on the point; but if so, it was forgotten that I had made it an express condition that the privilege of a plurality of votes should be annexed to education, not to property, and even so, had approved of it only on the supposition of universal suffrage. How utterly inadmissible such plural voting would be under the suffrage given by the present Reform Act is proved, to any who could otherwise doubt it, by the very small weight which the working classes are found to possess in elections, even under the law which gives no more votes to any one elector than to any other.

While I thus was far more obnoxious to the Tory interest, and to many Conservative Liberals, than I had formerly been, the course I pursued in Parliament had by no means been such as to make Liberals generally at all enthusiastic in my support. It has already been mentioned how large a proportion of my prominent appearances had been on questions on which I differed from most of the Liberal party, or about which they cared little, and how few occasions there had been on which the line I took was such as could lead them to attach any great value to me as an organ of their opinions. I had moreover done things which had excited, in many minds, a personal prejudice against me. Many were offended by what they called the persecution of Mr. Eyre; and still greater offence was taken at my sending a subscription to the election expenses of Mr. Bradlaugh. Having refused to be at any expense for my own election, and having had all its expenses defrayed by others, I felt under a peculiar obligation to subscribe in my turn where funds were deficient for candidates whose election was desirable. I accordingly sent subscriptions to nearly all the working class candidates, and among others to Mr. Bradlaugh. He had the support of the working classes; having heard him speak, I knew him to be a man of ability, and he had proved that he was the reverse of a demagogue by placing himself in strong opposition to the prevailing opinion of the democratic party on two such important subjects as Malthusianism and personal representation. Men of this sort, who, while sharing the democratic feelings of the working classes, judged political questions for themselves, and had courage to assert their individual convictions against popular opposition, were needed, as it seemed to me, in Parliament, and I did not think that Mr. Bradlaugh's anti-religious opinions (even though he had been intemperate in the expression of them) ought to exclude him. In subscribing, however, to his election, I did what would have been highly imprudent if I had been at liberty to consider only the interests of my own re-election; and as might be expected, the utmost possible use, both fair and unfair, was made of this act of mine to stir up the electors of Westminster against me. To these various causes, combined with an unscrupulous use of the usual pecuniary and other influences on the side of my Tory competitor, while none were used on my side, it is to be ascribed that I failed at my second election after having succeeded at the first. No sooner was the result of the election known than I received three or four invitations to become a candidate for other constituencies, chiefly counties; but even if success could have been expected, and this without expense, I was not disposed to deny myself the relief of returning to private life. I had no cause to feel humiliated at my rejection by the electors; and if I had, the feeling would have been far outweighed by the numerous expressions of regret which I received from all sorts of persons and places, and in a most marked degree from those members of the Liberal party in Parliament with whom I had been accustomed to act.

Since that time little has occurred which there is need to commemorate in this place. I returned to my old pursuits and the enjoyment of a country life in the south of Europe, alternating twice a year with a residence of some few weeks or months in the neighbourhood of London. I have written various articles in periodicals (chiefly in my friend Mr. Morley's *Fortnightly Review*), have made a small number of speeches on public occasions, have published the *Subjection of Women,* written some years before, with some additions * * * * and have commenced the preparation of matter for future books, of which it will be time to speak more particularly if I live to finish them. Here therefore, for the present this memoir may close.

THE END

SELECTED BIBLIOGRAPHY

OTHER WORKS BY JOHN STUART MILL

A System of Logic, Ratiocinative and Inductive, 1843
Essays on Some Unsettled Questions of Political Economy,
1844
Principles of Political Economy, 1848
The Enfranchisement of Women, 1853
On Liberty, 1859
Dissertations and Discussions, 1859, 1867, 1876
Considerations on Representative Government, 1861
Utilitarianism, 1863
Examination of Sir William Hamilton's Philosophy, 1865
Auguste Comte and Positivism, 1865
The Subjection of Women, 1869
Three Essays on Religion, 1874

BIOGRAPHY AND CRITICISM

Anschutz, R. P. *The Philosophy of J. S. Mill.* New York
and London: Oxford University Press, 1953.
Bain, Alexander. *John Stuart Mill.* London: Longmans,
1882.
Borchard, R. *John Stuart Mill: the Man.* London: C. A.
Watts & Co., Ltd., 1957.
Britton, Karl. *John Stuart Mill.* London: Penguin Books,
1953.
Davidson, W. L. *Political Thought in England: the Utili-
tarians, from Bentham to J. S. Mill.* New York: Henry
Holt & Company (Home University Library of Modern
Knowledge), 1916.
Halévy, E. *Growth of Philosophical Radicalism,* 2nd ed.
London: Faber & Faber, Ltd., 1934.
Hayek, F. A. *John Stuart Mill and Harriet Taylor; Their
Correspondence and Subsequent Marriage.* Chicago:
University of Chicago Press, 1951.

Leavis, F. R. Introduction to *On Bentham and Coleridge*. London: Chatto & Windus, 1950; New York: George W. Stewart, Publisher, Inc., 1951.
Mueller, I. W. *John Stuart Mill and French Thought*. Urbana, Ill.: University of Illinois Press, 1956.

A NOTE ON THE TEXT

The text is based on the first edition, published in 1873 by Longmans, Green, Reader, and Dyer. The spelling and punctuation have been brought into conformity with modern British usage.

INDEX